Ethnicity&Equality

France in the Balance

AZOUZ BEGAG

Translated and with an introduction by
Alec G. Hargreaves

University of Nebraska Press | *Lincoln and London*

Publication of this book was
assisted by a grant from the
National Endowment for the Arts.

A Great Nation Deserves Great Art

Library of Congress
Cataloging-in-Publication Data
Begag, Azouz, 1957–   Ethnicity and
equality: France in the balance /
Azouz Begag; translated and with an
introduction by Alec G. Hargreaves.
p.   cm.   Includes bibliographical
references and index.
ISBN-13: 978-0-8032-6262-1 (pbk.: alk. paper)
ISBN-10: 0-8032-6262-0 (pbk.: alk. paper)
1. France—Social conditions—1995–
2. France—Ethnic relations. 3. Marginality,
Social—France. 4. Minorities—France—
Social conditions. I. Title.
HN425.5.B345   2007
305.5′6094409045—dc22
2006023736

Set in Minion by Bob Reitz.
Designed by A. Shahan.

Contents

Translator's Introduction

In the fall of 2005 widespread disorders broke out in disadvantaged neighborhoods of Paris and other major French cities. Prominent among those who took to the streets were minority ethnic youths who torched thousands of cars and attacked police stations and other public buildings. The political controversy generated by the disorders quickly pitted the ambitious center-right interior minister, Nicolas Sarkozy, against a new member of the government, Azouz Begag, France's first-ever cabinet minister of North African immigrant origin. Angered by Sarkozy's dismissal of disruptive youths as *racaille* [scum], Begag insisted on the need to understand the long-standing social and ethnic tensions in which the disturbances were rooted.[1] Just days before joining the government in June 2005, Begag had, in fact, completed a manuscript in which he conducted precisely such an analysis, laying bare the festering social and ethnic injustices that only a few months later were to plunge France into its most serious civil disturbances in almost forty years. In the wake of the riots Begag complemented the typescript with a preface highlighting the intimate connections between those disorders and the deep-seated malaise that he had analyzed just a few months earlier. It is that manuscript, previously unpublished, that is presented here, translated into English.

Begag, a leading sociologist and best-selling novelist, has for more than twenty years been researching and writing on the evolution of French society in the light of immigration from former colonial territories. He has also lived that evolution personally since his birth in 1957 to Algerian immigrant parents in the city of Lyon. His childhood years in a shantytown there were described in his autobiographical novel *Le Gone du Chaâba* [Shantytown kid], first published in 1986.[2] His work as a sociologist has been constantly informed by his unfettered access to disadvantaged minority ethnic groups concentrated in stigmatized urban areas commonly referred to as the *banlieues*. It was here that the disorders of 2005 erupted. Just as, in his literary and sociological writings, Begag had drawn extensively on his firsthand knowledge of the banlieues, so, while Sarkozy sent in the riot police to quell the disorders, Begag threw off his security escort to walk unaccompanied and unannounced through the burning hoods in order to see for himself what was happening. What he saw confirmed what he had written only a few months earlier: that entrenched socioeconomic inequalities compounded by widespread ethnic discrimination and decades of political neglect had bred a subgroup of disaffected youths whose resentment was such that they were ready to erupt into violence at the slightest provocation.

These youths—mainly teenagers and almost exclusively male—can best be understood as part of a third generation among minority ethnic populations rooted in immigration from former French colonies, especially those in former French North Africa, a region also known as the Maghreb. The first generation—migrant workers (mainly male) and their spouses—began settling in France in significant numbers during the 1960s. The second generation, born in France of immigrant parents, reached adulthood during the 1980s, when those of North African origin—among them, Begag—became known as *Beurs*. The third generation have been born in France since the mid-1980s. Not all of the third generation are of Maghrebi origin; growing numbers are of West African, Caribbean, or other non-European ancestry. Neither are they all in the strict biological sense third generation, that is, the grandchildren of migrants. Some are the children of migrants who entered France as recently as fifteen or twenty years ago, while others are the youngest children of older migrant parents with large families in which the age gap between the oldest and the youngest children can in some cases be twenty years or more. What distinguishes this third generation is that, unlike the first two, it has never known anything other than the ethnically stigmatized environment into which it was born, and many of its members are convinced that there is no hope of their ever escaping from the banlieues.

Migrants, by contrast, regarded France as a land of opportunity, one that they frequently compared with their country of origin, to which (paradoxically in some ways) many dreamed of returning. As children, the second generation saw their migrant fathers defined by the jobs they had found in a French economy experiencing labor shortages during a period of rapid economic growth. When they came of age in the 1980s amid the onset of rising unemployment, this second generation had a reference point from which to hope for better prospects, and many believed that, if they used the rights of citizenship that they (unlike their immigrant parents) enjoyed, they could advance in French society. But, with the almost uninterrupted rise of unemployment experienced in France during the final quarter of the twentieth century and the disproportionate impact of this arising from discrimination against minority ethnic groups, the third generation, which grew up during the 1990s, has had neither the firsthand memory of a worse past (the poverty of their parents' or grandparents' country of origin) on the basis of which to count their blessings nor the memory of a better past (a period when jobs were plentiful) to serve as a reference point for future hopes. Instead, theirs is the flat horizon of teenagers who have seen their fathers and/or older brothers largely excluded from the labor market and can see little if any reason to suppose that better prospects await them.

It is on the members of this third generation that Begag focuses in this new book. To describe them he invents the neologism *jeunes ethniques* [young ethnics], which served as the title of his original manuscript. The innovative use of the word *ethnic* as a noun rather than as an adjective signals both the pertinence and the peculiar role of ethnicity in shaping the experiences of these youths when compared with the generations that preceded them. Before moving to France migrants internalized the cultural norms of their home country, which they would attempt to transmit to the children they were to raise in France. Possessing a strong sense of ethnic identification with their country of origin, they were hampered in their efforts to transmit those feelings by limited cultural skills (most Maghrebi migrants, for example, were illiterate) and by the preeminence of majority ethnic cultural norms in French educational, media, and other institutions, which deeply affected their children, weakening their identification with the homeland of the older generation. Among the grandchildren of migrants, familiarity with the cultural heritage of the land from which their ancestors came is weaker still. But this does not prevent them from being ethnicized by members of the majority ethnic population, in whose eyes swarthy skins, Arabic names, or other signs of non-European ancestry are regarded as synonymous with layers of cultural alterity that necessarily place those concerned outside, if not, indeed, in outright opposition to, mainstream French society.

This kind of ethnicization, in which majority ethnic observers project onto minority ethnic youths barriers that are more imagined than real, is apt to become a self-fulfilling prophecy, for those who are stigmatized in this way may be tempted to respond by displaying hostility toward those who reject them, even if they have little or no alternative sense of belonging beyond the confines of their local neighborhood and only the loosest of affiliations with the homelands of their migrant ancestors. It was precisely this kind of self-fulfilling prophecy that erupted on the streets of the banlieues in the fall of 2005.

While widespread, those disturbances did not involve the active participation of all those categorized by Begag as *young ethnics*. Among this generation Begag distinguishes three separate subgroups, the first of which he calls *dérouilleurs*, a neologism derived from the verb *dérouiller*, meaning "to de-rust or loosen up." A literal translation of *dérouilleurs* would be "de-rusters"; a less awkward translation would be "movers." Members of this subgroup, to which Begag devoted an earlier book, have much in common with what others have called the *beurgeoisie*, that is, a socially successful segment of the Beur generation (second-generation Maghrebis), typified in many ways by Begag himself.[3] Dérouilleurs are characterized by their success in breaking out of the limited horizons associated with stereotypical images of the banlieues. They were not involved in the disturbances of 2005. The primary actors in those events were members of a second subgroup of young ethnics, whom Begag calls *rouilleurs* [lit. "rusters"], that is, disaffected young people who, in contrast with the galvanized dérouilleurs, remain where they are and rot. Rouilleurs, on whom this new book focuses, are characterized not only by their lack of social and geographic mobility but also by low levels of cultural capital, which limit their capacity to think critically and/or laterally. Unable to construct complex personal and/or social relationships, rouilleurs are, thus, in multiple ways cut off from the wider society within which they reside in marginalized banlieues. If a literal translation of *rouilleurs* would be "rusters," the disaffected and disconnected nature of those in this subgroup might be better conveyed by characterizing them as *disjointed*. Rouilleurs are disjointed both internally and externally, unable to construct a purposeful project beyond the confines of the banlieues and detached from, if not outright hostile toward, the dominant institutions of French society while nevertheless sharing many of its values.

The members of the third subgroup, labeled by Begag as *intermédiaires*, that is, those in an in-between position, are undecided in outlook, neither firmly committed to moving beyond the social marginalization into which they were born nor irremediably convinced that they are destined to remain permanent prisoners of majority ethnic stigmatization. The long-term future of young ethnics and of their relationship with French society as a whole depends in many ways on the direction in which members of this intermediary subgroup head, toward either incorporation or disconnectedness. More immediately, it is on the rouilleurs, the disconnected young ethnics, that Begag focuses here.

Significantly, the chain of events that sparked the conflagration of 2005 began with a police identity check on a group of young ethnics in Clichy-sous-Bois, in the northeastern banlieues of Paris. Minority ethnic youths have long complained of harassment by the police, who in their eyes symbolize a repressive and discriminatory social order. Disproportionately high rates of police identity checks on young ethnics typify the suspicion with which they are regarded by many members of the majority ethnic population. Fear of harassment has, in turn, generated deep distrust among young ethnics such as those who, in Clichy-sous-Bois, fled and took refuge in an electrical substation rather than submit to a police identity check. When two of them—of Mauritanian and Tunisian origin, respectively—died there by accidental electrocution, many in the banlieues were quick to blame their deaths on aggressive policing and took to the streets to demonstrate their anger by torching cars and attacking police stations and other public buildings. Within days, the cycle of police repression and counterprotests spiraled into the most serious civil disturbances seen in France since 1968.

At first sight there may appear to be no obvious connection between those events and the personal anecdote recounted by Begag at the beginning of his manuscript. His crossing of the Franco-Swiss border after a television interview in Geneva about his career as a writer may seem far removed from the daily lot of young ethnics in the banlieues. On closer inspection, they share a highly significant feature: the instinctive suspiciousness of many French officials faced with people of non-European, especially Arab, appearance. In the face of ingrained prejudices that appearance is sufficient to trigger discriminatory treatment that the personal merit or social success of an individual, invisible on his or her face, is powerless to prevent. The customs officers who stand between Begag and his native country, France, are directly comparable with the police officers whose daily harassment of young ethnics in the banlieues stoked the resentment from which the urban conflagration of 2005 sprang. Unlike the middle-aged Begag, whose professional and other successes enable him to rise above such humiliations, teenagers caught in dead-end lives in the banlieues are prone to explode in destructive outbursts of anger.

The identity checks that sparked the disorders of 2005 are deeply symbolic not only of the role played by the police in enforcing what young ethnics see as a discriminatory social order but also of the wider pattern of identity politics to which the ethnicization of social differences has given rise. In the eyes of young ethnics the disproportionate rate at which they are asked to produce their identity papers is symptomatic of deep-seated suspicions among many members of the majority ethnic population concerning the legitimacy of their presence in French society. Checks on their papers enable the police to scrutinize not only their names but also their nationality and/or immigration status and, by the same token, their right to be in France. In point of fact the overwhelming majority of young ethnics, including those who took to the streets in 2005, were born in France, and, as the children or grandchildren of immigrants, they are automatically French nationals who, by the same token, have the inalienable right to reside in France.[4] The disproportionate rate at which young ethnics are subjected to identity checks reflects the reluctance of many on the majority ethnic side of French society to acknowledge that young people of color and/or of Muslim heritage really belong in that society. Suspicions and prejudices of this nature fuel patterns of discrimination that exacerbate the socioeconomic inequalities to which postcolonial minorities are prone by virtue of their disadvantaged backgrounds. Discriminatory notions of national identity are, thus, intimately linked with socially divisive identity politics.

Divisions of this kind permeate the discourses of both majority and minority ethnic actors. As Begag notes, on the majority ethnic side a seemingly value-free word such as *Arab* has long been contaminated by pejorative connotations, which were rife during the colonial period and are still present today. Similar deprecatory undertones are often present in majority ethnic usage of words such as *Muslim* and *immigrant*. Politicians on both the Right and the Left of the political spectrum are by no means immune from the use of stigmatizing language. The socialist Jean-Pierre Chevènement, who served as interior minister from 1997 to 2000, referred to unruly youths in the banlieues as *sauvageons* [lit. "wild children"], which many read as a scarcely disguised echo of colonial disdain for *sauvages* [savages], that is, supposedly uncivilized non-European peoples.[5] The disturbances of 2005 were fueled in part by anger in the banlieues at the use of the word *racaille* by Nicolas Sarkozy to describe young troublemakers there. Sarkozy's remark had been made during a visit to Argenteuil, in the northern banlieues of Paris, on October 25, two days before the deaths of the two teenagers in Clichy-sous-Bois, but the two events were reported more or less simultaneously.[6] As Sarkozy already had a reputation for provocative language—a few months earlier he had vowed to "nettoyer au Karcher" [clean out with a power washer] troublemakers in another Paris banlieue—it is probable that many in the banlieues thought that he had used the word *racaille* to describe the youths who had taken to the streets to protest the deaths in Clichy-sous-Bois. In remarks made by youths interviewed in the media, anger over his language was frequently cited as a significant factor in the rapid escalation of the local protests in Clichy-sous-Bois into nationwide disorders. Pressed repeatedly to retract the term *racaille*, Sarkozy declined numerous opportunities to do so, though, had he wished, he could easily have distinguished between the youths to whom he had applied the term before the events in Clichy-sous-Bois and those who took to the streets there two days later. Instead, he stated: "Voyous ou racailles, je persiste et signe" [Hoodlums or scum, I stand by every word].[7]

Like other stigmatized groups before them, minority ethnic youths in France have sought to turn the tables on their detractors by inventing their own counterdiscourses. In some cases this involves proudly and sometimes aggressively reappropriating a stigmatizing label, endowing it with positive instead of negative connotations. Just as, in the late 1960s and early 1970s, African American activists proclaimed, "Black is beautiful," so in a number of cases minority ethnic youths in France have made a point of publicly calling themselves *Arabs, Muslims, natives,* or even *racaille.*[8] Another strategy has been to invent new labels untainted by majority ethnic usage. A well-known example of this is the word *Beur,* a self-designating neologism first adopted in the 1970s by second-generation Maghrebis in the banlieues of Paris as a *verlan* [back slang] inversion of *Arab.*[9] In more recent years young miscreants in the hoods have proudly called themselves *caillera,* a back-slang version of *racaille.* In other cases minority counterdiscourses have taken nonverbal forms, as in the ostentatious display of Muslim beards and prayer beads or ritualized forms of street violence such as confrontations with the police and the torching of cars, designed to demonstrate the limits of dominant power structures.

Confrontational behavior of this kind could be taken to signify fundamental rejection of dominant values and social mores in France. As Begag shows, this would be a very superficial reading of events. The young men who torch cars or engage in other forms of abuse or incivility, such as displays of disrespect for schoolteachers or macho behavior toward young women, are motivated by anger at their exclusion from a society in which they wish to share, rather than by the attraction of an alternative social or cultural system. It is true that, in some cases, their disappointment and anger can be such as to lead them to invest their aspirations and energies in alternative value systems, such as radical forms of Islam. But it would be wrong to read cases of this kind as evidence of a fundamental tendency of minority ethnic groups toward forms of community formation that are customarily demonized in France as *communautarisme* [ethnic separatism or factionalism]. Numerous studies by sociologists and other researchers have shown that, in general, second- and third-generation members of minority ethnic groups identify with the cultural norms dominant in France—as seen not only in the primacy that they attach to the French language but also in their adherence to values such as individualism, secularism, and equality of opportunity—far more closely than with the heritage of migrant parents or grandparents from very different cultural traditions.[10]

For the last twenty years, political discourse in France has been dominated on both the Right and the Left by the supposed need to protect what is habitually termed the *republican model of integration* against the alleged danger of communautarisme. On this view of things alien cultures introduced into France by immigrants, especially from the Islamic world, threaten to give rise to separatist enclaves if the Republic fails to impose on all citizens and residents a uniform set of norms or, worse still, if it officially acknowledges the existence of ethnic and cultural differences. In reality the dangers of communautarisme have always been grossly exaggerated, not least because the public education system and the mass media in France have consistently infused into second- and third-generation members of minority ethnic groups a far greater attachment to French cultural norms than to the cultural baggage of their immigrant forebears. That is why, as Begag notes, the notion of *integration* rings so hollow in their ears. For many on the majority ethnic side the endlessly stated need for "integration" has been a coded way of saying that people of minority ethnic origin must give up the cultural differences supposedly blocking their absorption into mainstream society. In reality minorities have been prevented from participating in French society not by their cultural differences but by the prejudices and roadblocks placed in their way by members of the majority ethnic population.

In their misplaced obsession with the imagined dangers of communautarisme, French politicians have until recently refused to recognize the day-to-day importance of racial and ethnic discrimination in limiting the opportunities of minority ethnic citizens. In so doing they have failed to honor the promises of the Republic, enshrined in its motto of "Liberty, Equality, and Fraternity" for all, first proclaimed in the Revolution of 1789. Many politicians argued that, as racial discrimination was banned in both the constitution of the Fifth Republic and a law passed in 1972, the problem had been dealt with and/or it would be a socially divisive step for the state to explicitly concern itself with ethnically characterized forms of social behavior. As a result prosecutions for racial or ethnic discrimination have been extremely rare.[11] The supposed incompatibility of republican values with a vigorous antidiscrimination policy, including arrangements for measuring differences in the treatment accorded ethnically defined groups, has created a void in which, over a long period, everyday acts of racial and ethnic discrimination have gone largely unchecked, breeding enormous frustration and disaffection in the banlieues. The violence to which this disaffection gave rise was, thus, a consequence, not of communautarisme, but of the Republic's failure to live up to its own principles.

If Begag pulls no punches in laying blame where it is due, he refuses to despair of the Republic. The problem, as he sees it, lies, not in a supposedly innate tendency toward minority ethnic communautarisme, nor in what disaffected young ethnics may be tempted to see as fundamentally false republican principles, but in convincing all parties that the way forward lies in a more honest assessment of the current situation in France and more earnest attempts at turning republican values into practical realities. If, as Begag suggests, the Republic needs to be reconstructed, this does not mean abandoning its principles. On the contrary, it means recognizing the de facto salience of ethnic differences in the same way that the Republic has in the past recognized the need to address social and gendered differences. It means making space less grudgingly for the full diversity of the national population, in particular by ensuring genuine equality of opportunity for all citizens.

The French experience in this field is marked by a vocabulary that is not always readily translatable into English, though many of the issues to which it relates are also present in the English-speaking world. In translating Begag's text a pragmatic approach has been adopted, using English equivalents where these are faithful to the original meaning, while retaining the original French expressions where these serve to convey the specificity of the situation in France and/or where literal translations could be misleading. For example, the word *ban-*

lieue has been retained, while other closely related expressions, such as *cités* and *quartiers sensibles*, have been translated. While *banlieues* is, on one level, a generic term for "suburbs," in everyday usage during the last twenty years it has become synonymous with particular types of outlying urban areas, namely those characterized by high levels of social disadvantage and minority ethnic settlement. These are the equivalent of what, in the United States, are commonly referred to as the *inner cities* or *ghettos*. As their French equivalents tend to be located in the outer reaches of cities, rather than close to the downtown area, it would be misleading to translate *banlieues* as "suburbs," which in the United States connotes comfortable middle-class neighborhoods. As there is no comparable risk of confusion in the case of *cités* and *quartiers sensibles*, these have been translated as "housing projects" and "hoods," respectively.

One further feature of the text should be noted. When Begag presents himself as a sorcerologist (*sic*) or claims to believe that the earth is flat, he is, of course, speaking tongue in cheek. One of the hallmarks of his writings, both literary and sociological, is the creative and playful use of language, making extensive use of puns, neologisms, and irony, including self-mockery. This kind of wordplay exemplifies his belief in the importance of seeing things from more than one perspective. As he shows in one of the anecdotes recounted in the text, humor requires the mingling of ideas or viewpoints that, because they cut across each other, would ordinarily be regarded as incompatible. Humor may not resolve such contradictions, but it does render them more manageable. In a similar way the image that Begag proposes of equal opportunities as a system of differential gears holding the nation on the road does not eradicate diversity but enables people of different origins to work harmoniously together. It is in that spirit that Begag seeks to renew and reinvigorate the fundamental values of the Republic.

APRIL 2006

Author's Preface

When I became minister for equal opportunities in June 2005, I did not know that the government in which I had agreed to serve would be faced a few months later with the most serious civil disturbances seen in France in almost forty years. But, when the disorders broke out in the fall of 2005, I knew what lay behind them, for, shortly before entering the government, I had painted a portrait of the young men from whose ranks the rioters were to come and invented a name for them: *jeunes ethniques* [young ethnics]. That portrait, based on my work as a sociologist and many years of firsthand experience in the disadvantaged urban areas known as the *banlieues*, lay at the heart of a book manuscript that I completed in May 2005. When I gave the typescript to my friend Alec Hargreaves, he proposed to translate it for English-speaking readers, and I immediately agreed. Neither of us imagined that, even before the ink was dry on the translation, the government in which I was about to serve would be forced to declare a state of emergency in response to widespread attacks by groups of young ethnics on police and public buildings in the banlieues. Yet those attacks came as no surprise to me, for they were rooted in the alienation and anger that I had highlighted among young ethnics toward the more favored and powerful parts of French society.

I call these youths *young ethnics* because they are the children or grandchildren of immigrants from former French colonies who have been stigmatized by members of the majority ethnic population, many of whom feel that people of non-European origin do not deserve to be treated as equal members of French society. Young ethnics are, in that sense, ethnicized. But this does not mean that they are themselves motivated by a desire to perpetuate an ethnic or cultural identity inherited from their immigrant parents or grandparents. On the contrary, they are far more attached to the material values dominant in French society than to the Islamic heritage of migrant forebears from former French colonies in North or West Africa. During the fall 2005 disturbances, a number of prominent intellectuals and politicians blamed the disorders on Islam. Such claims were quite unfounded. The police, intelligence services, and mainstream media all reported that there was no evidence of an Islamic agenda among the rioters. Where Islamic organizations intervened, it was to urge an end to the violence, not to stoke it. Few, if any, of the rioters said that their aims were Islamic. In fact, very few of the rioters were quoted in the mainstream media as saying anything at all. This was not simply because mainstream journalists lacked contacts among young ethnics. More fundamentally, it was because the young ethnics who had taken to the streets were generally poorly educated and lacked the training, experience, and leadership with which to articulate a coordinated set of demands. Exactly as I had said in the portrait I had painted, their frustration over ethnic discrimination and social marginalization was such that they were liable to erupt into violence at the slightest provocation, especially if it came from the police. When two of their number died while fleeing a police identity check and the government minister in charge of the French police described disruptive youths in the banlieues as *racaille* [scum], their seething resentment exploded in cities throughout France.

The task we now face is to reconstruct the Republic. That reconstruction is a double process. We must first understand how the Republic came to this pass and then find the tools with which to repair it.

French politicians have often prided themselves on the supposedly unique virtues of their "republican" model of integration, which they have frequently contrasted with the ills attributed to so-called Anglo-Saxon (i.e., American and British) approaches to "race" relations. The events of 2005 demonstrated the illegitimacy of this arrogance. As a citizen, as a writer, and as a sociologist, I have learned much from the United States, especially where the experiences of minorities are concerned. As a teenager at junior high school in my hometown, Lyon, the first book that moved me to tears was *Uncle Tom's Cabin*. Its poverty-stricken and generous African American protagonist reminded me of my father. And in reading *Uncle Tom's Cabin* I also recognized myself for the first time as a person of color, though I already knew that I was an Arab—and, of course, French. In the 1980s I was one of many young people of North African origin in France who found inspiration in the American civil rights movement of the 1960s. In 1983 Martin Luther King's nonviolent campaign for equal rights directly inspired what became known as the Marche des Beurs, the first nationwide demonstration for equal rights by young people of North African origin, popularly known as *Beurs*.

Unlike the United States, France never instituted slavery on its own soil. But in parts of France's colonial empire slavery flourished until 1848, almost as late as in the United States, and in other colonies, such as Algeria, right through until the middle of the twentieth century, France practiced forms of institutional racism that were similar in spirit to segregation in the American South. It was to escape the poverty and injustice of colonial Algeria that, in 1947, my father left his native village near the city of Sétif to seek better economic opportunities as an immigrant worker in the French city of Lyon. His trajectory was not dissimilar to the Great Migration of African Americans in the early part of the twentieth century, which took them from the rural South to Northern industrial cities such as Chicago and Detroit.

When desegregation came in the United States, opening the way for policies of integration and, later, affirmative action, the effects of those policies were felt not only in the South, where racism had been institutionalized by the state, but also in the North, where other forms of discrimination were present. When, at almost exactly the same time on the other side of the Atlantic, decolonization in the South brought an end to institutionalized racism in North Africa and other former French colonies, no comparable measures were taken to address racism in the North, in France itself. No one at that time expected that France would become the home of sizable immigrant minorities originating in former colonies. And, when those minorities did settle there, politicians in France went into denial. Those on the extreme right—Jean-Marie Le Pen and the Front National—denied that those minorities had any right to be in France and called for their forced repatriation to North Africa. More mainstream politicians called for their integration, but on the condition that they became, in effect, invisible. They could stay in France provided that they became so completely French that no one would notice them. They did become French, both in terms of citizenship and to a large extent in terms of culture. Yet, no matter how French they became, their swarthy skins and Arabic names made them the targets of widespread discrimination by members of the majority ethnic population. For many years, mainstream politicians denied or minimized the existence of ethnic discrimination. As the Republic's constitution and laws banned discrimination, the matter was considered closed. Yet what good is the theoretical principle of equality, consecrated in the motto of the Republic ("Liberty, Equality, Fraternity"), if in practice it is flouted every day in the lived experience of countless citizens?

Only recently has it been acknowledged that the failure to enforce antidiscrimination laws has called into question the credibility of the republican credo. As minister for equal opportunities, I have been attempting to close this gap through the Equal Opportunities Law of 2006, which provides better job opportunities for young people in the banlieues and gives new teeth with which to enforce antidiscrimination laws.[1]

The measures now being taken will not solve at a stroke the problems that, sadly, have become endemic in French society. It will take years to repair the consequences of decades of political neglect. During the period immediately following the Second World War, the French enjoyed what they came to look back on nostalgically as *les trente glorieuses*, thirty glorious years of economic expansion and near full employment. During that period economic migrants were actively sought in response to labor shortages in France. Many came from colonial or former colonial territories in Africa and elsewhere. The economic slowdown that began with the oil shocks of the 1970s gave rise to what I call *les trente calamiteuses*, thirty disastrous years of high unemployment and economic insecurity in which the children and grandchildren of migrants, especially those originating in the Islamic world, were treated as suspect or illegitimate parts of French society. It is now time to inaugurate *les trente prometteuses*, thirty promising years for which it is our responsibility to prepare the way by removing the obstacles and injustices placed in the path of minority ethnic citizens. A France that turns its back on diversity is a nation unfaithful to the principles of the Republic. A Republic that embraces and celebrates diversity is the harbinger of a richer and stronger France.

FEBRUARY 2006

Ethnicity and Equality

Introduction

Welcome to France

I love Switzerland. One morning, I arrived cheerily at the train station in Geneva with my usual Arab face and little black briefcase. The previous evening I had recorded an interview for a literary program on Swiss television about my much-commented-on success story in French society. Now I was ready to take the 10:30 train back home to Lyon. The sky was blue except for a few clouds in the east.

At 10:15 precisely I presented myself at the French customs post through which passengers had to pass before boarding the train. My only luggage was the little black plastic briefcase that I had picked up at a recent conference on the topic of "frontiers" at the University of Toulouse. It contained a few overnight toiletries and three books. Following in line behind a mixture of French and

Swiss passengers, I entered a narrow corridor at the end of which two customs officers, one male and one female, were taking a close look at the people filing past them. A third officer was holding on a leash a dog trained in the detection of drugs. I moved forward. I bade a routine good day to the inspectors; then suddenly, just as I was about to move past their gaze, they both ordered me to halt and blocked my passage by standing in front of me as if a drawbridge had suddenly dropped down. I stopped dead, then smiled. For a moment they seemed a little embarrassed to have acted in exactly the same way at exactly the same moment. Their professional reflexes were no doubt primed to sniff out suspicious characters like me. With an ironic exclamation I made light of their overzealous synchronization and let them do their work. The woman started asking me questions. Looking me straight in the eye, she asked if I had anything to declare, valuables or sums of money exceeding seventy-five hundred euros. Looking her straight back in the eye, I immediately replied that I had nothing of any kind to declare. Otherwise I would have done so . . .

Now came a heavy, innuendo-filled silence. She seemed to be wondering what to do next. Should she believe me and let me go on my way or dive in, indicating that she had doubts? I could see her eyes focusing on my little briefcase. She asked me the purpose of my visit to Geneva. I said that I had been invited to appear on Swiss television to talk about my work as a writer. My poor little briefcase was still in her sights. I said my train was due to leave in ten minutes. She finally made her mind up and, feigning interest in my literary career, politely asked me to follow her to a cubicle so that a search could be conducted. She opened my briefcase. She ran her fingers through the books and a few papers, opened my toiletries bag, closed it again, then opened an empty envelope stuffed in among everything else. There were no banknotes and no drugs. She closed my briefcase and looked at me. I didn't say a word. Then, with the same meticulous professionalism, she asked to see my wallet. I jumped. My wallet? But I don't have a wallet! I never carry one. All I have is my identity card to prove where I'm from. The customs lady was surprised. Well, well, a passenger without a wallet. Strange, very strange . . . So where does he keep his money? Another long, heavy silence. To my astonishment she pushed her luck further and asked if she could feel my overcoat. I felt furious. She was determined to uncover the little something her razor-sharp flair had instinctively sensed was there. Her fingers worked through the pockets and every nook and cranny of my coat. Nothing. She was forced to give up.

There were only a few minutes left before my train, so there was no point getting angry. So why on earth did I suddenly explode? I couldn't restrain myself any more. I told the lady that, since she had asked about my work, she might be interested to know my politico-literary specialization was, in fact, antidiscrimination policy, if she could see what I meant. She remained unmoved. No, she couldn't see what I meant at all. So then, overwhelmed with anger, and trembling with rage, I shouted that I had just been awarded the Legion of Honor by the president of France and that . . . But she simply shrugged her shoulders. So what? Did that excuse me from the same border checks as everyone else? By now I was choking with rage. "That is not the issue, Madame. What I'm telling you is that the swarthy-skinned suspect whose plastic briefcase you've just searched has been publicly honored by the nation and won't hesitate to make use of that distinction to draw the attention of the public to the dirty little discriminatory practice to which you've just submitted him." I pointed out that she and her colleague had both reacted simultaneously when they saw me and that their clumsy synchronization indicated an intolerable type of profiling. It was no coincidence, I shouted, that the only person pulled out of the line was me, the only *Beur* [second-generation Maghrebi], complete with regulation swarthy skin. That was exactly what I shouldn't have said to her. Her colleague came up. I whispered that I felt ashamed for them, the way their arbitrary, capricious, and utterly irrational inner alarm bells had been triggered by my foreign-looking face. Annoyed by these impertinent remarks, the customs lady took my identity card and disappeared into an office from which she re-emerged two minutes later. She gave the card back to me. I supposed she must have taken a photocopy. She was determined to show me that she was the one who held the power, notably that of making me late for my train. I had two minutes left. Nursing my wounded Legion of Honor, I took back my identity card and ran for my train. I leaped aboard just as the doors were closing.

I was on my way back to France, on my way back home. Could I really call it home? I felt disgusted. I told myself to forget all about it and drop the matter; there was no point spending my life fighting such stupidity. I slumped in my seat and drank the bitter cup to the end. I was tired. Maybe I was paranoid, but in that case every other swarthy immigrant and the swarthy sons and daughters of every swarthy immigrant had the right to be paranoid too. As the train followed the meandering gray waters of the Rhône, I nodded off. "Bellegarde!

Bellegarde! Two-minute stop!" The name of the town awoke me with a start. "Belle Garde!" [On Guard!]. It was a sign. I sat up in my seat. Yes, I would keep up my guard. No, I wouldn't keep quiet. I wouldn't let the matter drop. My name is Azouz, diminutive of Aziz. I am a French citizen, born in the third arrondissement of Lyon, and regard myself as the spiritual son of the 1789 Declaration of the Rights of Man and of the Citizen. I loathe racism and discrimination, and I want to live free from such scourges. I'll make sure that there's an inquiry into the behavior of the French customs officers at the train station in Geneva. I know perfectly well that they'll deny the facts, that they'll claim that I was treated "just like everyone else." My complaint won't get anywhere. In spite of that, I write my complaint and send it off, like a bottle thrown into the ocean, an act of resistance.

1   Fear of the Police

A Foggy Night in the Rue de la République

This book may seem to have gotten off to a bad start, but I want to continue and get to the heart of the matter by recounting another anecdote that is really quite poignant. As the son of an Algerian immigrant, I've always been afraid of the police. I always felt a natural, instinctive fear rooted in a distant past that went way beyond me. One evening recently I was in a street in Lyon, and something suddenly happened that changed the whole picture. It was when I suddenly realized that some police officers blocking my path to conduct an identity check looked like . . . children! At any rate, they looked so young for police officers that I felt I must somehow have lost track of time. It was as if I'd suddenly moved on to a new stage in my life. I looked at myself and thought:

I'm nearly fifty, I'm getting "old," and by the same token I have no need to worry about the police excesses or racist insults from which I suffered so much as a teenager in the housing projects where I lived. That evening these young police officers made me realize I wasn't frightened by them at all. I no longer felt like an automatic suspect in the eyes of French society. The ghosts by which I had been haunted had left me and gone to plague someone else. My "integration," as the phrase goes, had now entered a new phase. I told myself it was now time to lead the rest of my life free from the burden that I had carried until then of being seen as a foreigner and feeling like a victim.

Then, one evening after dark, a young woman in police uniform waved me down, stopped me, and came up to my car. I can't now remember whether I bade her good evening. In any event, in what seemed like a panic-stricken voice she abruptly asked me whether I could see any "fog" outside. Surprised, I immediately thought that there must be a fire and assumed that she had become tongue-tied in her panic, saying *fog* when she had meant to say *smoke*. So I looked through my windshield, and stuck my head out the side window, but saw no trace of fog. "You don't see any fog?" the young woman repeated. "No, sorry . . ." I wished I could have helped and was trying to offer to do so when she interrupted me and barked: "Well, switch off your fog lamps!"

For a few seconds I was dazed. I couldn't understand what was going on. My mind oscillated between thinking I must have misheard and fearing I had heard only too well. She must have been twenty-five. Sheepishly I came to the conclusion that I had correctly heard what she had shouted at me. My hands started fumbling around the dashboard in search of the wretched fog-light switch, which I had, of course, never used. She pointed abruptly to the switch, as if to say: "Is this car really yours?" I pressed the button, and an orange light went out. She then invited me unceremoniously to move on. I drove off. Then I stalled. I could see her shaking her head at the sight of such an incompetent driver. Fortunately I managed to start the motor again. After driving a hundred yards, I burst out laughing. OK, it was a nervous laugh. But I realized that I had refrained from telling her that I was an adviser to the minister of the interior, Monsieur Dominique de Villepin, with the mission of promoting equal opportunities in the police service. If I had told her that, she would most certainly have felt ill at ease, and I don't like making people feel ill at ease. It also occurred to me that she might not have the faintest idea who Dominique de Villepin was.

When I got back home, in a narrow street in the Arab quarter of Lyon, I still felt agitated.[1] I felt bitter and sick. Why had that young policewoman talked to me so discourteously? What image of *me* could she have had in her head to talk so disrespectfully to a citizen such as me? Who was *I* for *her*? Someone just passing through, obviously, a foreigner not from these parts, someone quite unconnected with locals like her. I was some floating fellow whom she could hurt, make fun of, vent her hatred on along with whatever personal anxieties she happened to be feeling, all with impunity, for such a fellow could have no means of recourse since, by definition, no one knew him and he knew no one. Who would believe him if he went into a police station and said that a policewoman had mistreated him? Who would give credence to his word, the word of an unknown outsider, against the sworn testimony of a police officer? This was the lesson I drew from my nocturnal encounter: the police-woman had taken me for Simmel's "stranger," an Arab migrant who'd arrived yesterday and would be on his way again the next morning.[2] To whom could I complain about what had happened to me?

When my parents arrived in France a few years after the Second World War, they were treated the same way. Now, after half a century, nothing had changed! It was perfectly reasonable to feel bitter. In native eyes I was still an immigrant worker. Alone at home I found myself slipping into a minidepression. In an effort to counter it I tried as usual to laugh, but it didn't work. So I lay on the sofa, turned on the TV, and watched a recording of France playing some foreign team or other. After a while I realized that my eyes couldn't figure out who was who: there were so many foreigners, so many colored players on both teams that I couldn't see who was on which side. All I could see was colored players everywhere. Profiting from this confusion, my mind returned to my altercation with the policewoman, and I smiled maliciously as I thought again how she could never have imagined that I had written a report on equal opportunities for the minister of the interior. Maybe she might never know. I had been right not to mention it, thus sparing her a psychological trauma that might have haunted her for the rest of her life. I said to myself: Maybe one day she'll find herself watching TV and then, what a surprise, what a misfortune, what a catastrophe, when she sees me with the minister, remembers the incident over the fog and the stalled car; then at last would come a redeeming moment. Her eyes would come out of the mist and would see things differently, from a changed perspective. She would never see things the same way again in the rue de la République. From now on she would tell herself that behind every swarthy face there could be someone important, someone capable of causing serious trouble for her if she were to treat him the way she did me that evening. Her idea of public service would, thus, be transformed.

Why This Mess?

So the young policewoman had taken me for Simmel's stranger, the Other. Whose fault was this? To some extent hers, but not only hers.

During the 1960s immigration from the South was seen as a flow of temporary workers with no families, camping in the margins of the host society, which was thought to have no need to worry about them because they were *not there for good*. Family reunification was a gradual, almost imperceptible process in cities up and down France. At first the children born to immigrants in France seemed silent and invisible in the shadow of their shantytown shacks, then later in the playgrounds at the foot of their housing project tower blocks. They seemed to live apart, "among themselves," without any cultural interaction with the French, simply waiting for the day when they would return home.

Then suddenly, in the mid-1970s, "their" presence among "us" became an issue with the first waves of the international economic slowdown brought on by the spectacular rise in oil prices driven by OPEC's major oil-producing Arab countries. Now their presence was seen as a problem in the schools of residential neighborhoods, in public spaces, and, in due course, in prisons. Simultaneously the labor market became inhospitable for "immigrant youths," to whom at one time employers had looked to replace their aging parents in insecure jobs that nobody else wanted to do. Anti-Arab racism and social exclusion became the norm. In the public imagination oil was associated at one and the same time with Arabs and with unemployment. These lines of thought became so intertwined that Maghrebis [North Africans] ended up being blamed for unemployment and scapegoated for the economic downturn. Anti-Arab racism took on alarming proportions. Some of the "immigrant youths" began to go off in their own direction, turning against the authorities, and triggering a violent policy of repression under the presidency of Valéry Giscard d'Estaing. The police stepped up their presence in the zups [housing projects] where these young people lived. Thousands of them would soon see the inside of police stations, courts, and prisons. Many were expelled from France, where they had been born, to the "home" country of their parents, where they had never previously set foot. Most came back to France illegally, living clandestinely in their hometown. It was during this period that they began to feel like the disowned, illegitimate children of French society. The grand mythical principles of the equality of all citizens before the law were trampled underfoot. Until the 1972 law prohibiting racism, discrimination against immigrants and their children went unpunished despite the French constitution's recognition of inalienable rights belonging to all human beings irrespective of race. Successive governments claimed that there was no need for a law against racism on the grounds that racism was virtually nonexistent. This occultation constructed a wall of silence behind which it was easy for all sorts of injustices to be committed against *les jeunes Nord-Af-*

ricains [young North Africans] in the housing projects, whom the police started calling *les N.A.*[3]

Beginning in 1976 young people in the ZUPs tried to organize themselves with the help of social workers, the growing number of clashes with the authorities having strengthened their collective consciousness. Relations with law enforcement officers worsened. This degradation was further aggravated by the racism of policemen "repatriated" from Algeria after independence in 1962, many of whom had been recruited into the law enforcement services of metropolitan France, where they set about settling old scores with the Arabs who had launched a war to gain their independence and had then come and installed themselves in France! Numerous incidents bear witness to the almost war-like atmosphere of this period. In 1977, for example, in Vitry-sur-Seine, in the southeastern *banlieues* [disadvantaged, multiethnic suburbs] of Paris, around thirty youths attacked three policemen as an act of reprisal for the harassment that they had been suffering. In 1979 and 1980 similar events took place in banlieues of Marseilles, Paris, and Lyon, where young people considered themselves to be at war with the police. In June 1979 a police sweep on young Maghrebis in Nanterre, in the northwestern banlieues of Paris, provoked the indignation of a group of lawyers, who took up the case with the justice and interior ministers. "In the interests of security" the police had arrested dozens of youths, some of whom were under thirteen years old, but all of whom were visibly Arabs; none of their French friends was arrested. All the "suspects" were photographed and placed on police files.[4]

The same year brought serious confrontations between young people and the police in the banlieues of

Lyon.[5] The zups of Vénissieux–Les Minguettes, Rillieux, and Vaulx-en-Velin, which had just been built, contained dense concentrations of Maghrebi families who had been rehoused from nearby slums, temporary shelters, and shantytowns. France was becoming aware that living on its soil was a new generation born of immigration and colonization. As the children of foreigners, these youngsters were themselves regarded as foreign. Skirmishes with the security forces attracted growing media attention:

In Vaulx-en-Velin, a disadvantaged suburb of Lyon, seventeen-year-old Adbelkrim Tabet lived in the district of la Grapinière, where 40 percent of the residents were Maghrebis. He had already been taken to court several times for stealing mopeds and cars and had served several months in prison. In la Grapinière he was a local hero. He would taunt the police by driving past them on stolen mopeds. On September 15, 1979, a police patrol was ordered to arrest him. He was tracked down in an apartment belonging to some friends. Six or seven policemen, together with a superintendent, surrounded the apartment. Realizing he could not escape, the youngster slit his wrists. At the same moment a shot was fired, setting off pandemonium in the housing project. People started shouting that the police had fired at Adbelkrim. The rumor spread like wildfire and reached the apartment where the Tabet family lived. Adbelkrim's brothers, among them Azzedine, ran out, followed by other youths. Handcuffed and bleeding from his wound, Adbelkrim was led to the bottom of the tower block. The Maghrebis of la Grapinière, several hundred strong, gathered around him. As Azzedine approached his brother, fighting broke out. The police superintendent was grabbed and beaten by some of the other youths. Police reinforcements arrived, followed by firemen. Azzedine was taken away in a police truck. The tension reached boiling point. Bottles, bicycle frames, household garbage, and stones rained down on the police, thrown by youths, older men and women. The police retreated to the nearest police station.[6]

The year 1980 marked a turning point in worsening relations between youths of immigrant origin and the police. For the youngsters, the situation had gotten steadily tougher with heavy prison sentences, prison suicides, systematic deportations, and repeated attacks and murders in the hoods. That year the "Rock against Police" movement was created in Paris, modeling itself on concerts organized by young West Indians in Great Britain.[7] On April 19, a thousand young people from the banlieues of Paris assembled without official authorization on some spare land in the twentieth arrondissement to dance to the sound of music giving vent to their tough living conditions and their hatred of the police. It was a kind of forerunner of what would later become known as *rave* parties.

In April 1981, a hunger strike was begun by a Catholic priest, Christian Delorme, and a Protestant clergyman, Jean Costil, in a neighborhood of the Les Minguettes housing project in Vénissieux. They were demanding a halt to the deportation of youths of Maghrebi origin. Their demand was satisfied on May 10, when the Left won the elections and François Mitterrand became president of France. People in the ZUPs breathed again. There was a cease-fire. The five or six years of violence, repression, humiliation, and racism that they had just been through left a deep psychological imprint on an entire generation of youths of Maghrebi immigrant origin. Those years had shaken their confidence in French "hospitality." They had instilled attitudes of mistrust and defiance vis-à-vis the French police. From then right down to the present day families of Algerian origin in particular—among whom fear of French soldiers and gendarmes instilled during the colonial period has been passed from one generation to the next—have carried with them the violent heritage of the *grands frères* [older brothers] who in the 1970s were commonly called *les jeunes immigrés de la seconde génération* [young second-generation immigrants]. Visceral hatred of *keufs* [cops] has been inherited from the past. It will take time before the grandchildren of immigrants see law enforcement officers as being on the same side as they are. The wrongs suffered by the generation that preceded them engendered a collective memory that today's new generation of youths carries with it, ready to erupt at the slightest altercation with law enforcement officers.

Let me add a terminological note. Youths of Maghrebi immigrant origin know that police in the Brigade Anti-Criminalité [Anti-Criminality Brigade], widely deployed in the banlieues, call themselves the Brigade Anti-Crouilles, the word *crouille* being a derogatory term for *Arab*.

I Have a Dream

In a similar way to what happened during the 1960s in the United States with black desegregation movements, the 1980s were crucial in the identity formation of banlieue youths. For the first time they felt that they were recognized as a legitimate part of French society. They took to the streets in a new way, a space their parents had never claimed, whether in France or in their country of origin.[8] Emblematic of their new visibility in France was the 1983 Marche des Beurs [March of the Beurs], modeled on the 1963 demonstration led by the Reverend Martin Luther King Jr. in Washington DC. Horizons started to open. Among the *dérouilleurs* whom I met in 2001 while conducting interviews for a book, I often found echoes of this period, when youths of Maghrebi origin emerged from their rat holes as if after an aerial bombardment and forged a political vision of their presence in France.[9] Theirs was a long-term vision, breaking definitively with the short-term, temporary thinking of their parents and shallow-minded politicians. The impact of the *Beur* movement on the thinking and trajectories of individual dérouilleurs was unmistakable.

Back then, a generation ago, François Mitterrand and the Left won the hearts of the banlieues and of French youths of immigrant origin in the ZUPs by listening as they clamored to be heard by the Republic. This was an important turning point in the mental geography of many of these youths, for whom the skies of France finally opened.

A *turning point*: Yazid, director of a youth center in the Paris region, uses this expression when recounting his life in a fine autobiography. A juvenile delinquent with a prison record at the beginning of the 1980s, he would certainly have been deported from France had it not been for the mobilization of his family, social workers, and the mayor of his locality. Eventually he was put under house arrest. This was a key moment in his life. It gave him time to take a critical look at himself, to understand the realities of his past and present self. He recognized the importance of working hard, began studying, and took a new look at the people around him: "When you have people around you who understand you and who above all are ready to support you, you cast off the images of them you had before. . . . When you're a delinquent, you dislike certain people, but then you realize they are in fact good people."[10] In Yazid's case the people around him were able to help him change his mental representations of others. If an individual is to agree to modify his psychological outlook and adopt new patterns of social behavior, he must first of all trust his new instructors. For Yazid the transformation was radical. As for numerous other young Maghrebis of his generation, the electoral victory of the Left was a godsend for Yazid. Until then he had felt *guilty* in French society, illegitimate and out of place. After 1981 he heard a new public discourse on banlieue youths, more favorable to them, saw the deportations brought to an end and the right to form associations granted to non-nationals. He realized that he had, in fact, been a *victim* of a society that gave free rein to police racism toward people like him. Perceiving himself as part of a victimized community, he threw off his feelings of guilt. Later his new way of looking at things led him to study for a university degree in education. Today he is a member of a social therapy research team and studies banlieue violence. His autobiographical narrative is aptly titled *Repris de justesse* [A narrow escape].

In retrospect we can now see how deep, years later, was to be the disillusionment of these 1980s pioneers of a multicolored, open-skies France. The collective actions of those older brothers, constructive and democratic in spirit, have given way to stagnation, individualism, or, in the best of cases, individuality. Today we do not even have the words to clearly signify the people we are talking about: originally they were *jeunes de la zup* [youths from the projects]; then they were *jeunes des banlieues* [ghetto youths]; now they are *jeunes des quartiers* [youths from the hoods, i.e., "problem" neighborhoods]. The debate surrounding them is clouded by enormous terminological confusion. If we quickly review the main terms currently in use, notably in the media, we come up with the following typology, based on territorial, ethnic, religious, and temporal criteria:

TERRITORIAL REFERENCES
  jeunes des banlieues, or ghetto youths
  jeunes des cités, or guys in the hoods
  jeunes des quartiers, or guys in the hoods
  jeunes de la périphérie, or youths from across the tracks
  jeunes de zeps, or problem school youths[11]
  zonards, or dropouts
  lascars des banlieues, or wise guys in the ghettos
  jeunes des quartiers chauds, or guys from the hoods
  rouilleurs, or movers
  hittistes (*teneurs de murs*), lit. "young men leaning on walls," jobless and aimless
  indigènes de la République, or "natives" (i.e., non-European subjects) of the (colonial) Republic

ETHNIC REFERENCES
  jeunes d'origine immigrée, or youths of immigrant origin
  jeunes d'origine maghrébine, or youths of Maghrebi origin

jeunes d'origine arabe, or youths of Arab origin

jeunes d'origine arabo-berbère, or youths of Arabo-Berber origin

jeunes issues de l'immigration maghrébine, or youths of Maghrebi immigrant origin

jeunes issus des minorités visibles, or youths of visible minority origin

jeunes issus des minorités ethniques, or youths of minority ethnic origin

Arabes, or Arabs

Beurs, or second-generation Maghrebis

Rebeus, or Beurs

noirs, or blacks

renois, or blacks

blacks, or blacks

Franco-arabes, or Franco-Arabs

Franco-Algériens, or Franco-Algerians

Franco-Marocains, or Franco-Moroccans

TEMPORAL REFERENCES

jeunes de la seconde génération, or second-generation youths

seconde génération, or second generation

jeunes immigrés, or immigrant youths

immigrés de la seconde génération, or second-generation immigrants

descendants de colonisés, or descendants of colonial subjects

jeunes issus de l'immigration, or youths of immigrant origins

RELIGIOUS REFERENCES

jeunes musulmans, or young Muslims

jeunes arabo-musulmans, or young Arabo-Muslims

jeunes d'origine difficile,[12] or youths of difficult origins

In all there are around thirty different appellations, riddled with fallacies, contradictions, and ambiguities embodying the unease of the Republic vis-à-vis "citizens" who are not like "us."

Who and what are we talking about? It is no longer very clear. I remember a radio program in which I participated in Paris in December 2004 when I had just submitted my report on the promotion of equal opportunities to the minister of the interior.[13] The live broadcast was open to questions from listeners, and suddenly an exasperated listener in Nice tore into me on the air, screaming that he no longer dared even say the word *Arab* in everyday conversation for fear of being taken for a racist! His voice was trembling with anger. He complained that he no longer knew how to behave, how to complain about damage done in his neighborhood by *jeunes issus de l'immigration maghrébine* [youths of Maghrebi immigrant origin] without being treated as a racist. "We're not even allowed to call them Arabs!" he screamed at me. For him, that was the ultimate act of dispossession. He found the situation grotesque and intolerable: he was no longer *at home*, with the familiarity and intimacy where you can say whatever you want, whatever you think, about "foreigners" "sticking their *souk* [Arab bazaar] into your quiet, ordinary life," the same foreigners to whom you'd given jobs, social security, schools. Now the noisy presence of those Others was forcing him to adapt, think about the way he spoke and change. He couldn't cope with such a reversal, in every sense of the word. In his eyes, it was up to the others to adapt, not up to the people who belonged here. Not up to him. He concluded: "When we go to their country we don't expect them to adapt to us, do we?"

I let him carry on spitting it all out until the program presenter asked him to moderate his remarks, which were becoming openly racist, and which could, therefore, render him liable to prosecution. There are plenty of people in France who see "foreigners" in the same way. And no doubt plenty of people elsewhere in the world too.

So who and what are we talking about? In the course of compiling my *Arab's Shorter Dictionary* of terms used to designate youths of visible immigrant origin, I thought of an expression that I think hits the nail on the head: *jeunes ethniques* [young ethnics]. That is what it's about at root. After being publicly ethnicized for so long in the eyes of indigenous observers, these young people have decided to positively affirm their status as *ethnics*, in accordance with the relationship between "established" and "outsiders" as analyzed by Norbert Elias in his study of the logic of exclusion:

> The knowledge that by being noisy, destructive and offensive they could annoy those by whom they were rejected and treated as outcasts, acted as an added incentive, and perhaps, as the major incentive for "bad behavior". They enjoyed doing the very things for which they were blamed as an act of revenge against those who blamed them.[14]

This helps us get to the heart of the matter, but we are still not out of the woods. The adjective *ethnic* is the core issue. It is being used here as a noun. But it still does not tell us exactly who or what is being signified, for many of these young "ethnics" are protean free electrons with variable identities depending on where they are. If they regarded themselves as an ethnic minority as conventionally understood, it would be possible to conduct a study of their social behavior, but this is not the case. We are dealing with individuals whom the Republic has divested of their original cultural clothing and dressed in the tricolor tunic of French universalism, the fabric of which has suffered the erosion that myths habitually undergo together with other attacks from the virus known as reality. Today, just like the radio phone-in listener, young ethnics are on edge. They are in midstream, and the water is rising around them. They can see no reason to turn to politics or industry in search of hope. So where can they turn?

Before attempting to answer this question, let us consider more fully where they are coming from and what is now at stake as they seek a way forward.

2   Identity Comes and Goes

Let me return now to my Arab face, my black briefcase, and my detention at the train station in Geneva. It was a classic case of discriminatory treatment based on ethnic profiling of a type that is all too commonly experienced by people who appear suspect in the eyes of customs officers at international frontiers. To try to moderate my exasperation it might perhaps be argued that people crossing international frontiers inevitably sharpen suspicions and discriminatory reflexes, making these places inherently prone to racist excesses. What I mean is that people of color are not the only ones subject to more than their fair share of identity checks. Young people with tattoos or earrings or fluorescent tinted hair can also encounter prejudiced behavior. But this doesn't alter the fact that, since the terrorist attacks on the World Trade Center in

New York in September 2001, this is a bad time to be an Arab, an Arabo-Muslim, or a presumed Arab or Muslim.[1] This is all the more true when you cross an international boundary and arrive at U.S. immigration control with visas in your passport in the Arabic language, as I have done on a number of occasions. At the airport in Atlanta, Martin Luther King's home town, as at JFK in New York, it doesn't matter how many times I explain that I'm a French writer of Algerian origin, that I'm often invited to talk about my books in Arab countries, hence these visas. The immigration officers home in on those visas in Arabic, a language that they have seen Bin Laden and his accomplices using on the TV news, and that's enough for them to take me off to a special room for a special check. They're very sorry, they say, but it isn't their fault. After having already waited in line for an hour to get as far as the regular check, I now have to undergo additional questioning and waste a further hour or two surrounded by other "suspicious faces" from around the world. Who created this situation, making life so difficult for me? The American policeman says it isn't his fault. It isn't mine either. That's simply the way it is. I have to put up with it. I have to choke back my anger. Whatever happens, I mustn't rebel against the security system in American airports and the way it profiles certain travelers. These American policemen probably know that, until 2004, two French youths of Maghrebi origin brought up in the Les Minguettes neighborhood of Vénissieux were held prisoner in Guantanamo, following their arrest in Afghanistan. In their eyes am I not also a Frenchman of Arab origin? If I had had blond hair and blue eyes, would I have attracted their attention? Maybe not, but then my name would have struck a chord: Azouz, it sounds like Aziz, like Tarek Aziz, Sadam Hussein's (Christian!) foreign affairs minister. Sometimes that's all it takes to set off alarm bells at U.S. border posts. So I've made a decision: I'm going to change my passport. Although I have a passport valid until 2012, I think I'm going to pay for a new one so as to no longer trundle around with me these Arabic-language visas and in future pass more easily through passport control at Atlanta and JFK Airports—two names that, with my antiracist schooling, have a special resonance for me.[2]

Cachez ce visa arabe que je ne saurais voir! [Remove this Arab visa from my sight, for upon it my eyes should not alight!].[3] In France in the 1960s and 1970s—Martin Luther King was assassinated in Memphis in 1968—mutilation of their own identity was commonplace among youths of Maghrebi immigrant origin faced with constant discrimination because of their face or their address in an ethnically marked neighborhood. An entire generation grew up in the outlying areas of France's major cities living like crabs, with their bodies in one place and their minds in another. They were thrown out of gear by the feeling of not belonging *here.* I remember that, in the fifth grade at the Ecole Sergent-Blandan, in the historic heart of Lyon, a pupil of French origin insulted me by calling me *an invader.* I was petrified by this iniquitous accusation. For me invaders were people who came from another planet with misshaped fingers on a mission to invade the earth. Only David Vincent knew who they were! That was why they wanted to eliminate him. That at any rate was the story line in an American TV series in which I reveled during my youth. But it was crazy to suggest that my parents or I wanted to invade France! It was utterly absurd. I was born in Lyon. It was my home.

I wanted to explain to my classmate that he'd got the wrong guy. But there was no way of getting through to him. He punched me in the teeth and spat at me: "You're stealing the food from our [French] mouths!" A dark veil fell across my illusions of integration. I turned on my heels and ran home, my eyes filling with tears as I crossed the rue Gentil. I was traumatized. The truth was that I loved French food and ate as much of it as I could get. But, when I got home, I told my mom that from now on I wanted to eat only *khobz ed'dar* [homemade Arab-style bread]. "That's good," she said with a murmur of satisfaction, thinking that I was at last returning to my roots. This was a reassuring notion for my parents, who always wanted to think that I had never left them, that I was still part of what they were before, of everything that went before, that their children were part of a steady line of continuity stretching calmly on through time, history, and culture. I didn't tell her that I'd been hit by a French boy because I knew what her reaction would have been: she would have been frightened and would never again have let me venture out alone into the jungle of France.

This painful notion of being illegitimate children of France was transmitted from one generation to the next among young people of Maghrebi and African origin. It wasn't until many years after I left the Ecole Sergent-Blandan and the street bearing the same name, where I had lived at the time, that I found out who Sergeant Blandan was. What an irony it turned out to be! Pierre-Hippolyte Blandan was born on November 9 (I was born on November 5!) 1819 in Lyon. He enlisted in the army on January 14, 1837, becoming a corporal on August 6, 1839, and a sergeant on February 1, 1842. On September 9, 1837, his battalion was sent to Algeria, where the French were imposing their rule through military conquest. Between 1837 and 1842 he participated in all the major areas of fighting in the northeastern Algerian province of Constantine. These included operations against Ahmed, former bey of Constantine, and against various tribes in the region. Between 1841 and 1844 the Twenty-sixth Infantry Regiment moved backward and forward between Constantine and Oran—in the northeast and northwest of Algeria, respectively—to harass the enemy and resupply French positions. From June 29, 1841, onward the second battalion was in and around Algiers. Three companies were stationed in the town of Boufarik, from which, on April 11, 1842, a special convoy was due to leave for nearby Blida. To escort it a unit consisting of eighteen men, a corporal, and two cavalrymen was placed under the orders of Sergeant Blandan. The detachment set out. Near the Beni-Mered ravine it was ambushed. Sergeant Blandan was shot three times and killed. As he fell, he shouted: "Courage, my friends! Fight to the death!"

The day I learned the story of Sergeant Blandan I felt a strange combination of emotions. To think that he and I had been born in the same town, Lyon! To think that he had probably fought and killed some of my poor, defenseless ancestors in one of the tribes in the Sétif region, part of the province of Constantine. To think that, a century later, I went to a school bearing his name and learned to become French there. It was in that same school that I also had my first experiences of racism. What a curious historical twist this was.

Returning to the twentieth century, let us focus again on the 1970s, a difficult period for immigrants and their families. Amid all the economic difficulties of that time and the violent racism to which they were subject, why, one might ask, did they not return to their country of origin? Why did they put up with it all? The answer is simple: because the myth of their return had become precisely that, a myth. Deeply anchored in the minds of immigrants and their children, it had long enabled them to withstand the violent reflexes of rejection to which they were subjected in France. We felt a sense of pride and loyalty toward our parents' native country. That attachment led to many youths being deported across the Mediterranean when they fell foul of the law. This period of deportations gave birth to the Beur movement. Paradoxically, it was because second-generation North Africans had thus far retained the nationality of their parents and then taken to the streets to demonstrate against the injustices done to them that they became French! This too was a strange historical twist.

Today the balance sheet of thirty years of "integration" policy is pretty depressing for those of all political persuasions who believe in the values of the Republic. One might have expected politicians, especially those on the Left, to be forward-looking, to protect the rights of young people of immigrant origin, fight against racism, and ensure that they were treated with respect. It would have been good if the Ministry of Education had ensured that schoolchildren learned about the colonial period, the expropriation of land belonging to Muslims, the destruction of entire villages in colonial wars—and the real reasons for the presence of my friend Sergeant Blandan in Algeria. But a wall of silence was erected, and historical amnesia reigned. Gradually a deep division set in between politicians and everyday reality. In ethnically marked neighborhoods a certainty emerged: There was no point in hoping that integration would be handed to us as a gift. We would have to grab it ourselves. We would have to fight to win it, the way trade unionists and politicians had fought their battles. "Courage, my friends. Fight . . ."

What a bitter truth this is. In a democratic system that had placed equality at the heart of its constitution, we were entitled to expect greater intelligence and clearer vision in the construction of the French melting pot and the guarantees given to all of fair treatment. It was a particularly bitter truth to see that France had learned nothing from the struggle of Martin Luther King in the United States for a real policy of integration in favor of people of color. Here in our country, which likes to parade itself to the world as the home of human rights, patterns of discrimination have been allowed to develop, spreading their antirepublican bacteria and continuing today to threaten our national cohesion.

An Identity Reversal

Of course not everything in France is in bad shape today. There are encouraging signs that, despite everything else, processes of cultural fusion are actively at work. To give a seemingly anodyne example, ethnic diversity is so far entrenched in France that citizens of North or sub-Saharan African origin who have succeeded in society now write the whole of their first name on their business cards, whereas previously they simply put their initial in the hope of concealing their disadvantageous origins. In the 1970s, when I lived with my family in the La Duchère housing project, young Arabs would bleach their hair and eyebrows blond with peroxide in the hope of getting into discotheques from which they were habitually excluded. In pursuit of assimilation their motto was to look as white as possible. In 1952 the African American writer Ralph Ellison had published his famous novel *Invisible Man,* in which the black protagonist feels that the white majority refuses to see him or recognize his existence or humanity. Twenty years later young Arabs in France were trying to melt into the dominant whiteness in order to become invisible so that they would no longer be recognized and rejected on account of their origins. These were true revolutionaries in the spirit of 1789—veritable meritocrats!

What a contrast with today's realities! The self-denial in which the grands frères engaged has been replaced by a reactivated identification with minority ethnic origins, and Islam has now emerged on the scene as a rallying point in the sociological construction of a significant number of young Arabs. Now you can see in the hoods bearded young men and not-so-young men holding Muslim prayer beads in their hands, wearing white or gray djellabas, and sporting brand-name American athletic shoes. Not only are today's young Arabs no longer ashamed of themselves. They make a deliberate, ostentatious display of themselves as a kind of provocation, similar in spirit to a homosexual coming-out. This is a dramatic reversal compared with the self-effacement that predominated during the early stages of immigration, when the watchword among migrants was *celui qui garde fermée la bouche, ne risque pas d'avaler de mouche* [keep your mouth shut, and you'll keep out of trouble], signifying their avoidance of public visibility in the host society. Individuals were at that time reluctant to disturb the general order of things with their specificity, contaminating the seemingly perfect smoothness of public life and the pure uniformity of universal citizenship.

That time has now gone. Islam, ethnicity, and related claims to difference have now taken a seat at the table of republican values, filling the void left by the hollowness of the myth of equality and the principle of meritocracy. This movement has fed on a wider context of social disintegration, sharpened by successive waves of economic crisis, the chronic decline of values embodied in notions such as work, sustained effort, respect, and education, and loss of faith in politics as a collective project for society as a whole. After twenty years of the banlieues and of the vicissitudes of "integration" policy, it is clear that France has not lived up to expectations. The social cost of this accumulation of political errors is very considerable, and we are still paying the price of it. Now, if we look at the way in which society is developing as seen in the banlieues, in the cracks and critical gaps fissuring our society, it quickly becomes evident that territorial, socioeconomic, urban, and ethnic configurations look less and less like they used to. We have entered a period of unpredictable identity changes. The incantation of well-worn republican myths is to no avail. Every pore in the skin of French universalism is now coming out.

3 Disintegration

The eruption of the particular, of religiosity and ethnicity, into the habitual fabric of the Republic is closely linked with the ways in which urban structures have been evolving. Cities are paradoxical spaces, which seem to bring people close to each other while simultaneously generating isolation and social frustration. Cities create peculiar forms of violence. Marked simultaneously by centrifugal and centripetal forces, they are places of attraction and repulsion, integration and disintegration, social promotion and *déclassement*, proximity and distance.

Nevertheless, cities are public spaces that bring people together in ways without which citizenship would be impossible. By their density, they have always made it possible for individuals to see social space as unified and, thereby, to feel integrated. The language of urban living has been an important tool in the socialization of individuals, facilitating the mixing of differences, and enabling them to contribute to the social order through the visibility of a collective memory impregnated with social codes. In a word, as a vector for the regulation and integration of social, ethnic, professional, cultural, and other differences, urban spaces and their languages have historically helped construct the idea of democracy. They have helped build the political foundations on which civilizations are built. So we must view the current crisis in the banlieues and the associated fragmentation of space in relation to this breach in a long process of construction, a breach rooted in the exacerbation of individualism and the erosion of social cohesion. The participation of the individual in the social fabric—a place of distinction and at the same time of identification—is seriously weakened by the fragmentation of urban spaces.

Did a truly republican city of equal opportunities ever exist in France? Social exclusion has built walls, barriers, facades, and frontiers that are invisible to the naked eye but that are well-known to bus and taxi drivers and to providers of public services. One day, during a research interview, a Paris bus driver showed me a bus stop at the entrance to a *cité* [housing project] on the outskirts of the city, saying that from there people would get onto the bus without paying their fare and that there was no point putting in inspectors because they would make no difference. His tone of voice indicated that this part of town had its own laws. He was right. During the last twenty years I've researched in hundreds of similar neighborhoods, and I always have the same sensation of crossing a frontier when I enter them. When you leave the downtown area of a city and enter one of these neighborhoods, you no longer quite feel as if you are "in the city" any more, certainly not in a city of the Republic as conventionally understood in France. You are in a kind of wasteland, an uncertain zone. You are on the other side of the tracks. The landscape has changed: the verticality and the density of the habitat have replaced the horizontality of downtown and its immediate surroundings. There are boarded-up and broken windows and signs of squatters. Multicolored washing hangs from the balconies: sheets, carpets, and lots of children's clothes, families being larger here than in other parts of the city. On some of the balconies you can see mountain bikes and even scooters, a sign that no one feels confident leaving items of that kind outside at night, even in a garage—a sign too that people here steal from each other, the poor against the poor, the socially excluded against the socially excluded. Ground-floor and first-floor apartment windows are protected by wire meshing. Everywhere satellite TV dishes point like sunflowers toward a geostationary satellite linking the real-here to the dreamed-about-there. On this side of the tracks people are like stray molecules hovering around the nucleus of the old world. Here a multicultural society is busily fermenting. Each year brings something new: after an ethnic grocery store and a kebab seller comes a café-bar frequented solely by men, a halal butcher's, an ethnic hairdresser, a phone store for cheap calls to Algeria, Morocco, the Comores, Turkey, Mali, and Senegal, and a cybercafé.

Let's be clear about it: this is a multiculturalism cradled in poverty, amid the broken windows of dirty apartment block entrances, vandalized phone kiosks and bus shelters, and graffiti-festooned walls hurling insults at the police or announcing a demonstration. Sometimes, but not always, there is a police station nearby. In a neighborhood I visited on the outskirts of Metz in 2004, a new police station had just been inaugurated by the minister of the interior. It was protected by armor plating and video surveillance. The old police station had been burned down by youths amid street fights.

Although some exceptions to this pattern can be cited, the state of these neighborhoods makes it clear that the republican idea of the city has been gravely weakened by social exclusion and the desocialization of young ethnics. The violence associated with these neighborhoods is constantly present in the media. People are afraid of these places. There is no end to the rumors about them. "Things go on there," people say, contrasting them with quiet neighborhoods where "nothing happens," where there is no friction, where everything is supercool. Without any doubt media treatment of "urban violence" involving young ethnics has impeded the social integration of so-called Arabs, on whom urban disorders are blamed.

Racism on one side, counterhatred on the other, and fear everywhere. Social exclusion first concealed these young ethnics, then manufactured them, and finally propelled them onto the public scene. The development of segregation against Maghrebis and blacks has provoked racist reactions among them against the Franco-French. Their withdrawal into themselves has led to the cultivation of microterritories, sometimes down to the level of an apartment block entrance! Across the space of a generation each riot in a hood, each confrontation with the police, has ratcheted up the wall separating young ethnics from whites.

A Three-Phased Disintegration

How on earth did we reach this point? Since the Second World War there have been several different phases in relations between downtown areas and the hoods, or, to use Nobert Elias's terminology, between the city of the established and the city of the outsiders.[1] The first phase was one of indifference. During *les trente glorieuses*, thirty years of economic expansion between 1945 and 1975, industrial cities in France and other countries sucked in and digested workers, both indigenous and immigrant, as elements of the labor force spatially associated with shantytowns, temporary camps, and social housing. Then came a second phase, that of frustration. After 1975 spiraling unemployment had important spatial consequences: outlying islands of poverty sank ever deeper into economic insecurity, while downtown areas continued to accumulate wealth, making manifest great disparities in the degree of vulnerability facing different citizens and spaces in the face of the economic downturn. Then came a third phase, that of *la haine* [rage], graphically represented in the 1995 film by Mathieu Kassovitz bearing that title. Unable to control their frustrated desire to participate in consumer society, young ethnics in poor neighborhoods vented violent feelings of resentment against the system that excluded them. In France this third phase emerged clearly in the 1990s. It was accompanied by an additional feature: figurative suicide. During this period rioting by young ethnics often took self-destructive forms, morbid procession-like spectacles.

These rituals underscore just how far these youths are the product of an urban society that has destroyed the traditional family links and historical references that had previously sustained a sense of collective identity. It is almost as if the space in which they lived has become virtual; indeed, their very presence in that space has taken on a virtual quality. As the violence grew a self-preservation mechanism came into play: the banlieues started to drift off on their own, away from the shock waves of the system that had excluded them, and young ethnics started to reverse the logic of exclusion. At a previous stage they had been corralled in housing projects that came to resemble Indian reservations; now they began to champion these spaces as territories in which they could assert their autonomy and thirst for survival, at the same time introducing a new ethnic dimension.

Deep in the Reservation

Here now was a new definition of *integration*: finding a place in the system, but not at any price; now it would have to be a place in the sun. Like other young people of modest social origins a young ethnic is unable to find his place in society. For him, the city does not function as a space that brings people together. While physically present he is not really part of the city. He is trapped in a system that is constantly gathering speed, reinforcing his feeling of being left behind. His feeling of inertia is further strengthened by the illusion of mobility generated by television, notably through the bombardment of images of a world that seems constantly in movement and constantly changing. There is, thus, a feeling of being surrounded by movement while remaining stuck in the same spot, a bitter realization that others are moving while the young ethnic is not. Living in what amounts to a captive state is all the more schizophrenic when one has the impression that the world around one is accelerating but one cannot break out of the trap in which one is ensnared. With everything speeding up, speed becomes an object of desire in its own right, something to be exhibited as proof of one's participation in society. A symbol of power, speed also ministers to violent impulses. In the urban landscape of France this impulse finds its expression in the hoods. Etymologically, the Spanish word *rodéo* harks back to the American rodeo, a kind of fair at which cattle are branded, cowboys compete to show who is best at breaking in a horse, etc. This helps us understand what is happening when today cars are stolen and burned in the banlieues. Here, in place of a wild animal, a high-powered motor vehicle is captured for branding. The idea of taming and subjugating the object of this attention is omnipresent in this sacrificial ritual, as is the idea of death. This new-style rodéo is very precisely orchestrated. A young ethnic, alone or with accomplices, brings in his catch from the outside world, a powerful automobile in which he races up and down at high speed between the apartment blocks lining the avenues, screeches the tires, heats up the motor, shifts gears so as to break the gearbox (and your brainbox with it!), and, when the ceremony is over, smashes the car against a wall or some other obstacle before setting fire to it. The beast is, thus, branded and subjugated.

The arenas in which these ritual killings take place are the local neighborhoods in which the executioners live, where they are known and recognized. The ritual suicide of speed takes place in a safe haven, where the perpetrators know they are protected by their own kind and by the law of *omerta*. In these same places, children play in the streets, and working-class neighbors park the automobiles they have bought on credit. These arenas are far from the more classy downtown parts of the city. These are no Robin Hoods robbing the rich and the powerful to give to the poor. These are the gestures of poor people in the arenas of their own neighborhoods, and the ceremonies demonstrate how the exclusion of an individual is all the more frustrating when he is *physically* at the heart of a consumer society. He is situated geographically in that society but is deeply aware of being held outside it in a kind of void where he's allowed to look but not touch. The resulting frustration triggers uncontrollable desires, the "I want it all now" syndrome that is so common among young ethnics. With no training, no job, and no future, many of them have nothing to lose and are, therefore, inclined to pay back society with the violence it has inflicted on them. In the banlieues of the 1990s it became common to talk of la haine as a response to the unprecedented acceleration of social change running in tandem with isolation, ignorance, fear, and rejection of the *petit-blanc* [poor white] Other.

Cat and Mouse

Violence has undoubtedly been ratcheted up, but we must be lucid and avoid oversimplifying or confusing things. We need to see that the population of young ethnics is not a uniform bloc, as the discourses of rejection would have us believe. We can, in fact, perceive among them a dynamic typology composed of three main subgroups: *rouilleurs* [lit. "rusters," people who rot where they are]; *dérouilleurs* [lit. "de-rusters" or movers]; and *intermédiaries* [lit. "intermediaries," those in an in-between position].[2] These subgroups experience the relation between identity and territory in very different ways and are treated differently by the media. So far, in my references to young ethnics, I have, in fact, been talking mainly about the subgroup that I call *rouilleurs*, who are so heavily mediatized that they are often mistakenly assumed to represent young ethnics as a whole.

Rouilleurs are outside the normal social system. They depend for their living on a parallel economy fueled in part by drug trafficking. They have nothing to lose, and they set no moral limits on their behavior: they have no religion, no morality, no sense of civic responsibility, no fear. They are similar to some of the disaffected young blacks observed by James Baldwin in American ghettos in the 1960s.[3] In the consumer society in which they live these youths buy respect by displays of external wealth designed to counterbalance their interior void. This tension between interior and exterior is an important element in the notion of disintegration. Very visible socially, this group generates a lot of attention by feeding dominant media representations of the banlieues. These people, for whom *les cailleras*[4] has become a byword, engender feelings of rejection and exasperation among the general population. A recent sortie by this group took place in March 2005 during student demonstrations against government education reforms. After mingling with the demonstrators they beat up, robbed, and insulted petits blancs of their own age. The affair attracted huge media and political attention, pushing questions of ethnicity more firmly still onto the agenda of contemporary French society.[5]

In reality what is happening in France's *quartiers sensibles* [hoods] is on one level not much different from what is happening in other countries, both rich and poor, around the world. The social damage arising from the confusion of personal success with financial gain goes far wider than the banlieues and youths of immigrant origin. The questions of value at stake here could be summarized in the following terms: If we take young people living in poverty who have seen their fathers exploited as cheap labor, then thrown onto the scrap heap of unemployment, who have no culture, are completely depoliticized, are subjected to constant racism and are able to express themselves only through violence, how can we expect them to accept a temporary job for a thousand euros a month when they can earn that much in a day or two in the parallel economy? If this seems an aggressive question, it's because it brings us to the heart of the contradictions of a socioeconomic system in which money is the key to integration. What is happening today in the banlieues is the gradual breakup of a society that has placed money at the center of its identity and in which individuals are first and foremost consumers. In classical economics money was a means of exchange to facilitate transactions. Now it is an end in itself, something to be possessed for its own sake. For young ethnics it opens the door to the kingdom of the consumer society, the only space in which, by forcing their way through, they can gain the social recognition, power, and respect habitually denied to them and their parents as, indeed, in colonial times, to their ancestors. If you live in a banlieue and have *thune* [dough], a.k.a. *maille* [bread], you have the luxury of buying signs of seemingly boundless recognition in the form of brand-name goods that identify you as a can-doer. "I wear the brand": here we see the symbolic logic of the signs associated with goods such as Nike or Reebok athletic shoes, sold in Footlocker chain stores where growing numbers of sales assistants are Beurs and blacks. This implantation of fellow young ethnics within the Footlocker chain is designed to show that, in these stores, their money is accepted and their presence welcome. The same thing goes for the latest fashion in cell phones and in many other consumer goods, which young ethnics, both male and female, regard as key signs of social distinction. In such goods and the stores where they are sold they find a form of respect denied them elsewhere. Their money has the same value as that of whites. It has no smell. That isn't true elsewhere, notably in discotheques, from which they have been excluded for the last thirty years on the pretext that their presence would deter other, more creditworthy customers, whites in particular.

For young ethnics money represents more and more their passport to integration in the only world that matters to them in their daily lives, the world of the consumer. The way they talk about this suggests that they see society as a jungle in which anything and everything, including people, can be bought and sold. Among the most fragile this materialist obsession completely destroys any understanding of the work time that is required in order to earn money; it vaporizes any sense of long-term planning, patience, sincerity, or trust in human relations. They have no other way of thinking about their future other than as a financial projection. Here is how things now stand: young ethnics have understood that the consumer society takes into account only "guys who carry weight," in other words people who are economically significant. One of their expressions is *être blindé* [to be armor plated], meaning that you carry weight in the sense of having money but also in the sense of being protected from the vicissitudes of racism. For they know full well that money often enables people to overcome obstacles thrown up by racial discrimination. For example, people who have been discriminated against because of their nonwhite faces when looking for an apartment to rent know that, if they go into a realtor's office not as potential tenants but as property buyers and with cash to boot, they will be very respectfully received. Skin color or religious beliefs (real or supposed) don't then enter into social interaction because money doesn't have to state its origins; it is the true linchpin of universalism.[6]

This kind of logic is difficult to argue against when it is propounded by young people who have given up on their naive belief in equal opportunities. Let us not delude ourselves: this kind of thinking is doing enormous damage in the hoods. On several occasions in recent years while visiting certain neighborhoods with local residents as guides, I have been shown businesses based or presumed by my interlocutors to be based on drug money. My guides would whisper in my ear: "Ten years ago the owner of that restaurant was unemployed but drove around in a luxury automobile. Now he owns this restaurant. Where did he get the money?" These nouveaux riches have been able to accumulate and launder dirty money in local businesses. The youths operating successfully in this parallel economy represent a powerful countermodel to traditional republican values. I've heard it said that the nouveaux riches sneer at those who believed in the bullshit talked by conventional society, worked hard to earn a graduate diploma, then found themselves unemployed or serving at MacDonald's.

Practically every time I meet with people in the hoods I am asked questions of this kind about role models. How can I counter the harmful models to which they point? I have to give them an answer. I tell them that, besides the police taking appropriate action, those who have succeeded in society through education, hard work, humane values, and respect for their parents have a duty to disprove nihilistic rhetoric and to present themselves as more positive models for future generations. In a word we have to make dérouilleurs more visible.

Dérouilleurs are people in the hoods who have a stable job and income, future prospects, a good level of education, a stable family situation, a sense of citizenship, etc. In other words they are part of the French middle class. They are on the inside of French society and don't have any personal need for policies aimed at integrating them. By the same token they are in head-on opposition to the rouilleurs in their neighborhoods, whose behavior penalizes the general image of North and sub-Saharan Africans in those neighborhoods and in society as a whole. What really hurts the dérouilleurs is that they are almost invisible in media images of the banlieues. They are like trains that arrive on time. They are of no interest to the media because their behavior is quite ordinary. But they are there nonetheless and seem to be growing in importance; at least, in the last few years, associations and clubs have been springing up in France bringing together ethnically marked residents in their thirties and forties who are seeking to become more organized in order to change prevailing images of the community in which they originate. At an earlier time these young people played the game of institutionalized integration by creating associations governed by the law of 1901, enabling them to apply for public subventions. Now their philosophy is to seek social promotion through various forms of lobbying for what has become called *la beurgeoisie*.[7] In 2003–4 a network was even set up in Paris called Les Dérouilleurs. Other associations of a similar nature include 21ème Siècle and Africagora.[8] At root they are trying to copy the successful model of the Conseil Représentatif des Institutions Juives de France [Representative Council of Jewish Institutions in France], which is a frequent reference point for networks of French men and women of North and sub-Saharan African immigrant origin.

There is also a third group: the intermédiaries. They occupy a position midway between the rouilleurs and the dérouilleurs, hovering between two different social models. They are high school and university students, interns, short-term temporary workers, unemployed youths, etc., in search of stability, a firm point of anchorage, and a clear pathway to follow. Income levels are important for them and are all the more problematic in view of their young age, for they too are hypnotized by the consumer society and the brand names of American shoes such as Nike, the prices of which can reach £150 a pair when they check them out at Footlocker.

The fate of the hoods in the next few years depends to a considerable extent on what happens to these intermédiaries. Either they will find in the republican system the necessary tools with which to build a fulfilling future, thanks in part to the pioneering work of the dérouilleurs, or they will swell the ranks of the cailleras and of the prison population originating in immigrant communities and the hoods. If society proves unable to channel these precariously balanced youths in the right direction, the neighborhoods in which they are concentrated will become entrenched pockets of poverty with all the social problems that go with this. We can already see the effects of this process of ghettoization in a number of American and Third World cities, notably in Brazil and Colombia. So it's crucial that equal opportunities policy should target in particular these young people who are at a crossroads in their lives, looking for role models. We must encourage them to seek social advancement by placing their trust in the fundamental principles of the Republic. This is one of the reasons why France needs a vigorous antidiscrimination policy to protect young people from discrimination when they are looking for jobs and internships at the end of their schooling. Yet, in point of fact, in the high school streams where young ethnics are overrepresented (those preparing students for entry into the labor market with practically oriented school-leaver diplomas rather than for higher education), it has been well-known for years that it is often difficult, if not impossible, to obtain the necessary internships for them. It is when they try to find internships that their illusions evaporate, when they see their Franco-French classmates, but not themselves, being offered places. Some high schools now award them diplomas without internships so that they are not penalized. These students, who wanted to believe in the education system, see their prospects dwindling in the face of racial discrimination, and, when they return to their housing projects, they have no reason to serve as ambassadors for the rhetoric of equal opportunities. I recently heard of some high school students who had to take internships in kebab houses, the owners of which felt sorry for them and took them on out of ethnic solidarity. Realities of this kind engender among these young people feelings of humiliation and resentment against the system. We should be making much more serious efforts as a nation to counter this scourge.

This is no easy task. How can a company be forced to give internships to "students of this kind," defined on the basis of their supposedly bad reputation, religion, or origin? Even if the state had the necessary powers to fight such corporate practices, would-be interns suffering from discrimination won't like being forced on companies that don't want them. It's hard to imagine France importing the system of busing adopted in the United States whereby black students have been transported to schools in predominantly white neighborhoods in order to break down racial segregation. Forced integration of this kind seems unacceptably rigid. So what is to be done? Are we to allow despair and social disintegration to set in, or should we allow ethnic solidarity and factionalism to fill the gaps and repair the injustices generated by the failings of the republican system? There are signs of the latter tendency at the moment.

That tendency is gaining momentum as tensions rise between different communities of "us" and "them." In the fabric of our cities and of our schools the myth of social cohesion has been falling apart, and this trend has been accentuated with the identification of part of the youth population with Islam, especially in its radical forms. Here again we must be epistemologically subtle and avoid sensationalist oversimplifications. The typology outlined above is designed precisely to take into account the complexity of the parameters within which the future of the hoods will be forged. Depending on whether they identify with rouilleurs, dérouilleurs, or intermédiaries, individuals see their place in French society and the role they can play in it differently. For example, rouilleurs have an interest in cutting links between the hood and the rest of the town in order to isolate it. They build their identity in opposition to and rejection of Others. They derive feelings of power and dignity by inspiring fear in the rest of society, notably the police. That is why going downtown in force in that psychological disposition generates gratification.

Going downtown tells us a lot about certain forms of group mobility that I have often noticed among young ethnics, a mobility that was exemplified in the violence of March 2005 (discussed in chapter 6). Usually it takes the form of a gang of youths entering a shopping mall to taunt passersby and get attention one way or another. This behavior expresses a desire to gain the attention of the Other in key downtown spaces that are turned into arenas where youths from the hoods scare and confront whites. In this collective ritual the distance separating them from the rest of the city is turned into a form of social recognition and power: "We are in your part of town, and you're scared of us!"

Seeing the police arrive in force in the hood after a rodéo or a riot, as if entering a battlefield, is a way of demonstrating one's existence on the spot. Through a deliberate strategy of enticing police and firefighters into an ambush where their vehicles are stoned, the forces of order are humiliated in full view of the local inhabitants and television cameras. "We are in charge here! We may be a long way away from downtown, but we exist!" This is a way of taking a space of exclusion and turning it into a territory of collective identification, where social threads are woven by noise and agitation. That is how young men make tactical use of distance in the hoods, playing with and on the distance of separation and stress.

Young ethnics have become full-blown actors in the urban spaces of France. The days of *métro-boulot-dodo* [the daily work grind] have gone. Glancing back at the housing projects built in the 1960s and 1970s—Le Val Fourré, La Courneueve, Le Mas du Taureau, Les Minguettes—one cannot help but smile at the passivity of their inhabitants, basking in the functional comfort of their new apartments, far from downtown certainly, but waiting patiently at the stop for a bus to take them to work. At that time the geographic distance separating downtown from the zups was such that it made sense to speak of them as *dormitory suburbs.* Today that distance is manipulated in much more violent ways by young ethnics. Being far out doesn't mean keeping quiet. On the contrary the hoods are seething and simmering with tension, pulsating with energy in every direction. In the space of a generation the epicenter of urban sociology has taken the express metro out to the outer suburbs. It has even reached the point where a vast policy of urban demolition has been undertaken to reduce the social tensions generated by this habitat by giving it a gentler architecture.

Thirty years ago, in the La Duchère housing project, I lived with my parents on the seventeenth floor of a huge tower block from where I would often gaze at stunning landscapes on the distant horizon and at the foot of the building. On one side of the building were the Alps and Mont Blanc. On the other side were the hills of the Lyonnais region. Down below me was a parking lot, so far below that it seemed tiny. Some poplar trees had just been planted, and one day a strange question ran through my mind: would the trees eventually grow tall enough to reach the top of the building, almost 50 meters (130 feet) high?

My parents lived in that apartment until my father's death in 2002, when my mother left it.

A generation ago in La Duchère many of the youths from tower 260, where I lived, had served sentences in the Saint Paul de Lyon prison. Ironically many of the guards in that prison came from the same housing project. In the building where I lived a single elevator served the seventeen floors to which each ground-floor entrance gave access, some thirty-four apartments housing large families. It is not difficult to imagine how badly people on the top floors were affected by problems with the elevator, which often took an eternity to reach them. Problems of that kind helped sour relations between tenants.

At that time we had never even heard of what others called the *ascenseur social* [social elevator] and the social mobility that it symbolized. The junior high schools in our outlying part of the education system had so-called transitional classes that enabled youngsters to leave school as quickly as possible for low-skill jobs in a labor market that still offered full employment. We had never heard of the ENA (Ecole Nationale d'Administration) or Sciences Po (the Institut d'Etudes Politiques de Paris), exclusive training grounds for France's political and academic elites. Their names simply didn't exist in our local geography. The local *député* [member of the National Assembly] held court on Saturday mornings at the youth club to help guys find jobs with the city council in Lyon. I guess you could call him our elevator operator.

In my hood at the beginning of the 1970s there were *pieds-noirs* [white settlers from former French North Africa], Jews, *harkis* [Muslim troops who had fought for the French during the Algerian war of independence], Maghrebi immigrants, Italians, Spaniards, and Portuguese. There were also political refugees who had fled the Pinochet dictatorship in Chile. They brought us a breath of fresh air from far away. There was a Communist Party. There were trade unions. There were leaders who wanted to change the world. There were no drug dealers.

In my hood there was no Front National, but there was racism. With our Arab faces my buddies and I were refused entry to nightclubs.

In my hood, we talked about girls and never about religion. There was a synagogue but no mosque.

I recently went back to the hood, feeling nostalgic. To my great surprise the entrance was blocked. Walled up. My building, tower 260, was going to be demolished. All the inhabitants had been rehoused elsewhere. It felt strange to see the concrete giant shuttered up, emptied of its soul, cold and utterly silent, without a single car in the parking lot. There was not a single child to be seen. The building had been renovated at a cost of millions of francs only a few years earlier. How many ministers for urban affairs have held in their hands the levers of power in the space of the last generation? Four? Five? No one can remember exactly because there was never a clear path. There was no vision. All those ministerial comings and goings did nothing for the architectural coherence of a space in which thousands of people lived.

4   *I* Exists

A few years ago a chance professional encounter led me
to work with a group of French diabetes specialists on
the difficulties involved in treating patients of Maghrebi
origin, who account for a significant proportion of dia-
betics in France. This led me to study their relation with
time—time spent on culture, time spent on religion,
personal time—and on the possibilities of enabling doc-
tors to persuade them to adopt another temporal mode,
a form of temporal regularity for taking medicine, giving
blood samples, dieting in particular ways, etc. It seemed
clear to me that the challenge was trying to get Maghrebi
patients to take personal responsibility for treating their
condition. Their nurses and hospital caregivers made the
point that, in the families of these patients, the individual
was dispossessed of his or her illness, which was treated

as a matter to be handled by the whole community.

It is the same with death. When someone dies in the hood, the body no longer belongs to the family alone; it belongs to the community of believers, neighbors, and cousins. Death can never be a private matter in Islam. It is the same with happy events such as births. The problems arising from this are obvious when you see the endless family visits to which mothers and neighbors are subjected after a birth.

Cultural shocks of this kind arise from the different ways in which *private space* is understood in Maghrebi and French cultures. The frontiers between the private and the public are not the same. In Mediterranean families neither joy nor sadness is to be lived alone. The community naturally takes over the emotions of the individual. For example, anyone who has been invited to stay with a friend in the Maghreb knows how suffocating the host's hospitality can be. It's as if leaving the guest alone were an insult, a form of abandonment. "You want to be alone? But why? Don't you feel comfortable with me?" This type of social relationship shows that it's impossible for the host to imagine that his guest might want to go for a walk alone while "the family" is looking after him. Neither solitude nor the individual has any place in the social imagination of Maghrebis.

Similarly, when you are invited to share in a meal, there is a virtual obligation to eat—and to eat a further helping when you've finished what's on your plate! Even if you're not hungry, even at the height of the summer heat, you have to capitulate and eat. This widespread social practice shows that the personal well-being of the individual (who might, e.g., want to eat lightly) makes no sense in the cultural context of a family meal (where you must eat as expected). And you must eat a lot! For quantity is valorized in this culture, so much so that it will be said of a man (or a woman) who is slightly fat that he (or she) is in good health, whereas a slim or slender person will be judged to be sick. The more food, sugar, honey, semolina, he is offered, the more a guest knows he is being honored. Hence the enormous bottles of Coca-Cola and Fanta, full of fluorescent chemicals, served by Maghrebis with couscous and various meat dishes. It's as if it would be an insult to serve a couscous simply with water, which might be exactly what the guest is longing for! In an excellent sketch the French comedian Gad El Maleh asks with a deep Maghrebi accent: "What do you call someone who doesn't eat meat?" The answer is: "A pauper!" This joke gets everyone laughing because it is so solidly anchored in Maghrebi culture. You honor a guest with meat. The word *vegetarian* doesn't exist. Neither does the word *individual*.

That is why it is so difficult to administer a dietary regime based on clinical criteria to people molded in this type of culture, for their relationship to food is fundamentally shaped by social and cultural factors that set a primary value on hospitality. For Maghrebis, grand meals are part and parcel of public festivals, which are fundamental to the identity of the community. By the same token asking an individual to follow a special diet amounts to excluding him from that community. How could he accept an invitation and then not eat? Better to refuse straight out and live like a hermit! When conventional medical practitioners require a Maghrebi patient to follow their treatment, this is tantamount to tearing them out of their basic sense of identity. Culturally it is like giving them an artificial organ transplant. It is very difficult for a doctor to ask a Maghrebi patient not to fast during Ramadan because of diabetes, for during that month an individual is not an individual but a Muslim in spiritual communion with his Muslim brothers around the world. Fasting is part of that communion, and it is not to be broken in the name of some foreign medical treatment.

Health questions of this kind take us to the heart of the debate about the relation between individual and community, between private and public, in the way that time is represented and used. If there is a clash of civilizations between the North and the South, this is where it really lies: in the confrontation between "I" and "us."

How I Became a Sorcerologist

Besides my contacts with diabetes specialists, during the last twenty years I have had the privilege of receiving frequent invitations from youth clubs, social centers, local libraries, youth councils, and neighborhood associations in the hoods to speak about my research on immigration and social exclusion and about the role of the public education system, notably the acquisition of reading skills, in my personal trajectory. This has led me to work closely with the public school system in promoting *citizenship* through reading. One day I was speaking to a class in a ZEP (*zone d'éducation prioritaire*, i.e., a disadvantaged area containing schools targeted for special support) in the Le Mirail neighborhood of Toulouse, and a young student of African origin asked me the following question: "Monsieur, what do you do for a living?" I replied that I was a sociologist. His eyes almost came out of their sockets. He thought for a moment and said: "You are a sorcerologist? You do magic?" I laughed and then said that I was, indeed, a kind of magician, casting spells with ideas. The rest of the class sat there spellbound. Then I picked up an object, threw it into the air, and made it disappear. The young African was astounded. He smiled and asked me to do it again so that he could learn how to do it himself. He stood up, walked over to me, and begged me to do it again. Dazzled by my trick, he said that he wanted to be a sorcerologist too: that was what he wanted to do for a living. I asked him to return to his seat because his buddies were coming up to me as well and things were getting out of control. I told them all that a sorcerologist is someone who's escaped from a university and who uses his scientific knowledge as a source of power. The students were only half listening; they were still looking for the vanished object while I was trying to tell them to be wary of sociologists—and of sorcerers—because you couldn't necessarily believe everything they said. Then, in simple words and images, I started to explain what a sociologist does: he puts men and women into a kind of bowl and watches them living their lives, taking notes on what remains constant and what changes in their behavior. I enjoy explaining abstract things with concrete images. It's like turning concepts into a movie. Then I said that, to study the influence of new communications technologies on the lifestyle of my guinea pigs, I throw into the experimental bowl a cell phone or something of that nature. I know that children and young people in general like to see things so that they can grasp them through visual representations.

During the last twenty years I've had a lot of experience with these ethnic students and they way they see things: how they perceive themselves, the world around them, and matters such as humor and religious faith, phenomena that are at the intersection of reason and feeling, calm ratiocination and uncontrolled passion. I talk to them about the importance of the point of view from which you speak and the importance of learning a critical sense. To convey the importance of personal agency, I tell them in French: "Je n'*ai* pas réussi; je me *suis* réussi." This way of telling them that I've succeeded in life involves conjugating the French verb *réussir* [to succeed] with the auxiliary verb *être* instead of with the usual auxiliary, *avoir*. By turning it into a reflexive verb, one in which the agent is the same as the object, I show how "I" has been constructed by me. My "I" exists because of me. This means, for example, that I didn't become a construction worker like my father, that I avoided the fate that seemed to be reserved for me by social determinism. And I also freed myself from the community-based "us" that is fundamental to social relations in families of Maghrebi origin and that often destroys any attempt at carving an individual pathway.

Galileo? Never Heard of Him

One day at the Ecole Léo Lagrange, my primary school in Lyon, not far from the shantytown where I grew up, I learned that the earth is round and that it turns on its axis while circling around the sun. My teacher, Georgette, had brought into class a plastic globe on which we could see France, Algeria, the oceans and seas. I was fascinated to discover that the ground we lived on was moving! I was completely bowled over by this! My relation with the physical world, the sensory world, and the world *tout court* was turned upside down. Learning such a thing made a huge impression on me. The same evening I went home to the shantytown from school and went straight up to my dad, who could neither read nor write and scarcely spoke French, to share this amazing news with him: the earth is round and is circling constantly round the sun. He had just returned from work and was taking off the sheets of newspaper he used to stuff around his stomach to keep out the cold. He told me to turn round, just like the sun, then immediately kicked me in the behind and threw insults at me. How could I tell him such tall stories? What was the point of going to school if they taught you such stupid ideas? The earth was round? It circled round the sun? Whatever next? What a waste of time going to a French school only to end up as "dumb as my feet"!

I was struck dumb. I didn't know what to say except that my teacher, the source of all knowledge, had told me this and that I couldn't possibly doubt it. That evening I went to bed with nothing to eat apart from a piece of khobz ed'dar that my mother used to cook in the oven. My father was boiling mad. His son had fallen into the wrong hands at the French school and was on a downward path. Next morning he awoke me just as dawn was breaking, and we want to the window together to watch an extraordinary natural phenomenon: sunrise. There wasn't a cloud in the June sky, not the slightest haze to impair our vision. So my father and I followed the course of the sun as it crossed the sky. For hours we did nothing but watch the slow journey of the fiery ball across the vast expanse of blue. My mother brought us water and sandwiches without interrupting us, for we were engaged in real-time scientific observation, on which our concentration was completely fixed. At about ten o'clock in the evening the scarlet ball disappeared in the west, on the opposite side of the world from that at which it had appeared. My father drew our observations to a close, asking the dreaded question: Well? What had my eyes seen? The sun. So? I thought for a moment, then observed that it had moved all day! OK, so? I thought again and didn't know what else to say. He gave me a hint: What had my teacher told us in class? Oh yes, that the sun didn't move and that the earth moved around it! So? So she was a liar. And why was she a liar? I had no idea. I couldn't see why the teacher, who was so kind to me, would teach me things that were so completely wrong. I thought some more, in vain. Then my father explained: It was because we were Arabs, Muslims, poor immigrants! The schoolmistress didn't want to tell us the truth about the world because she and her superiors wanted to keep us in a state of ignorance and dependence so that we could never become more intelligent than they were, for knowledge was the key to power. Worse still: The French thought that the earth was turning beneath their feet because they drank too much alcohol and couldn't keep their balance (hence the expression *to be legless*). He had been able to verify this many times at the construction site where he worked, where a lot of beer was drunk. There was no need to seek any further for the truth, no need to heed the teachings of that charlatan of yore, Galileo. For my father there was only one correct way of going about things: look, observe, take the time to see the truth at firsthand. What had we seen with our eyes? We had seen the sun move in a curve across the sky. So the sun revolves around the earth and around us; when it is above our heads, it's daytime, and we work; when it's under our feet, it's nighttime, and we sleep.

How could I have been lulled into thinking that the earth turns round? Had not Allah given me a brain so that I could think for myself? Of course I should have asked the right questions, thought it out and asked myself how we could stand without falling over, how we could keep our balance on top of a huge revolving ball? How could we explain the fact that all the seas and oceans stay where they are instead of spilling out of their containers? Look, take an empty glass (a container), fill it with water, then turn it upside down. What happens? The water falls out, doesn't it? If the earth were revolving, the same thing would happen. There would be no water left in the Mediterranean, and we wouldn't be able to go on holiday to Algeria any more. This brilliant demonstration was chiseled in the hard facts observed by this man in the street, a peasant from the mountains of Kabylia who refused to be taken for a ride.

Obviously the earth is flat. For years now, in classes where ethnic kids are overrepresented, my demonstration that the earth is flat and that *we* (the ethnically separate *we*, Arabs, Muslims, immigrants) are the victims of a giant hoax by French teachers and the national Education Ministry (*them*, the Others, those *not like us*, *whites*) has found numerous believers. They almost all seem to believe this. Practically all these kids seem to be convinced that there is something suspect about the idea of the earth being round and revolving around a supposedly stationary sun; after all, we can see with our own eyes that the sun moves above our heads. They have been conned. When I tell them this, they look at each other speechless, full of confusion.

Occasionally, in classrooms where I'm busy sowing my subversive seeds, a student who isn't convinced by my demonstration raises his hand and claims that it's because of universal gravity that the earth can revolve while we stay firmly fixed on its surface along with our homes, the seas, and the oceans. When this new, abstract explanation is put forth, the other students pay more attention and hang on the lips of their classmate. I raise my eyebrows and say: "Universal force of gravity? What's that?" The tone of my question is designed to raise the stakes, forcing the student to push his case further. He replies that it is an invisible force, that it can't be seen but that he's heard it exists. I ratchet up: You can't see it? But shouldn't you believe only what you can . . .? The other students complete my sentence: . . . see! And that's it. Now the student who spoke up says that he was just relaying blather, things he'd heard said. He hadn't taken the time to distance himself from such rumors.

Obviously I am able to shake up received ideas in this way because of my position. Am I not a writer, a researcher with the CNRS,[1] someone who possesses knowledge, someone with the power to speak? In the course of their lives my young students have accumulated a body of knowledge in relation to which they have never really taken a personal position. Have they been able to see with their own eyes that the earth is round? No. So why do they think it is? Usually, at the end of one of these classes, some students come up to me and beg me to tell them the truth because they've seen on television that the earth is round and didn't the Americans send a rocket to the moon in 1969? The Americans? I shoot back, sarcastically raising the tone. They haven't *seen* anything; they've *shown* us things on television screens; they've made us swallow the idea that from the moon *they* can prove the earth is round. But you can't believe the Americans! Recently, for example, they tried to persuade the whole world to wage war on Iraq because its president supposedly had weapons of mass destruction that threatened the democratic world. History has shown this to be untrue. It was an invention, a pretext for going to war. So we shouldn't believe that they sent a man to the moon. As long as they are the ones with the TV cameras broadcasting images to the world, we can't believe what they say. On principle we should start by "unbelieving" them! That's a sure way to instill doubt and epistemological caution in my students, through down-to-earth questions that leave room for thought.

Sometimes students still can't make up their minds. They start up again with suggestions whispered in their ears by their teacher. Once again they ask the fascinating question: Is the earth round or flat? Pretending I can't hear, I make no reply, put on my jacket, ready to leave, and open the door while they look at me in frustration. Eventually I tell them I don't know whether the earth is round or flat and that I'm not really interested. This completely throws them. Then I say that the most important thing is to ask the question. You must ask yourself the question. And that's when it all becomes worthwhile because the students get a sense of what critical reasoning is like. I tell them that, if they want to find an answer to that fundamental question, there are libraries and books. They should go there in search of what they're looking for, in search of themselves, even if they don't find it. And I close the door behind me. I leave them wanting more. That way I think I've won. I win every time. My students are freer than Taliban children sitting cross-legged in madrassas in Kabul, holding the Koran in their hands, and hitting their heads with it as if to better fill their minds with it. My students are freer because I teach them the art of subversion and caution, I show them how to thwart the vice of preconceived ideas. I show them how to hold books at a distance in order to better construct their own point of view.

In the history of the human species nothing is ever definitively won, least of all the progress of scientific knowledge. My numerous encounters and dialogues in the hoods have led me to the conclusion that we need to constantly return to Galileo and Kepler through images and questions. We need to get back to basics and tackle fundamental questions in our daily lessons in civics, helping students discuss and develop arguments and personal ideas. The case of the earth's roundness illustrates the urgency of exposing young people to the history of thought, of ideas, and of democracy in its most basic forms. We need to tell children, not that the earth is round, flat, or oval, but why it is worth asking the question and seeking to answer it. Our young citizens need to be able to observe with their own eyes the course of the sun across the sky and to conclude from it that "what I see is perhaps wrong," what *my own* eyes *really* see is, perhaps, the opposite of the truth. In other words my eyes can be traitors to reality, imposters, and victims of hallucination. It is those kinds of intellectual gymnastics that need to be encouraged. They involve a movement toward abstraction, a change of point of view. I often make an analogy with another situation: when we're sitting in a train in a station next to another train and suddenly our train starts to move. We feel an unpleasant, dizzy sensation, for the train is moving, but we can't hear it moving, and everything in the compartment is motionless. Then, as we look through the window, we suddenly realize that it's the other train that's leaving, not ours. For a few seconds we were convinced our train was leaving, and we had a strange, dislocated feeling, with our bodies separated from our minds.

When we look at the sun, the same thing happens. I see it moving, but it isn't moving. I explain to my students that adopting a critical stance means being able to stand outside yourself, putting yourself in the position of the sun and realizing that "perhaps it's me and my eyes that are moving." Adopting a critical stance means putting yourself in the position of the Other.

All such fundamental questions make us giddy because they require us to distance ourselves from our certainties, from sensory organs such as our eyes through which we are used to perceiving the world, to consider them suspect and even refute them. Because this is hard, some students eventually say I'm "getting to their head," by which they mean I'm disturbing the mental habits in which they have gotten used to passively acquiescing. They say: Tell us whether it's true or false. They think that we, teachers and other possessors of knowledge, should take care of it between us, thus saving them time, effort, and the possibility of looking foolish. They want functional teaching with ready-made answers and immutable truths. Instead I defend my *point of view*, asserting that it's true *and* false at the same time, that the world is not binary in nature, that there isn't good on one side and evil on the other, as George W. Bush would have us believe, that they commingle, that life isn't on one side and death on the other, that the two are intertwined. I tell them that everything contains its opposite. I am fiercely opposed to simplifications of the world, society, or the individual, for they often lead to totalitarianism and radicalism.

Unfortunately my pleas for complexity are not as widely accepted as I would wish. For instance, when talking with students who are practicing Muslims, I tell them that there isn't *an* imam but that there are *imams* in the plural, that everything is a question of interpretation, that the reader's subjectivity is an important element in our understanding of a sacred text. I tell them that there isn't a lot in common between Indonesian, Chinese, Saudi, and French Muslims and that they may have a lot more in common with a buddy they've grown up with in the same housing project even if he doesn't have the same religion as they do. I tell them that, in my core identity, the religion transmitted to me by my parents occupies only part of the whole space. Many other parts of my mind are open, free, and liable to change. These are the spaces wherein reside tolerance and respect for everything that I am not. My identity is an entity in constant movement, constant motion. Like a nomad, it is always ready to packs its bags and go wandering. It is shaped by my identifications and my encounters. It is the journey through diversity that makes me personally rich. And, unlike plants, we human beings have the extraordinary capacity to move through space, to invent our own bearings and reference points through the uniqueness of our personal trajectory through geographic space. What human beings have in common is not such and such a characteristic but freedom, the capacity given to us all to change, as Rousseau would say. As we move, we change, for the landscapes and environments through which we pass change at every turn. In this way a human being discovers himself or herself and is discovered.

Is not one of the greatest frustrations experienced by human beings the loss of mobility? That is why prisons are called *maisons d'arrêt* [lit. "places of arrest"]. There your movement is arrested. I often go to such places to meet and talk with prisoners interested in my books. I always learn things from these meetings. On one occasion I had been invited to a women's prison and was in the process of developing my flat earth theory when one of the inmates dismissed my talk with a wave of her hand and said that in a consumer society what mattered was not the shape of the earth but having enough money to buy freedom. Her fellow prisoners agreed. As I knew she had a granddaughter, I said that, if one day the child asked her whether the earth is round or flat, it would be good to able to reply to her, wouldn't it? It was my way of talking about the transmission of social heritage and the positioning of knowledge in the continuum of History with a capital *H*. While apparently accepting this, she said that she put her faith in God. If she was in prison today, she thought, it was because the Almighty had wished it. It was her destiny. Such a way of looking at things was very far from mine.

Get Out of Yourself

By doubting what we are taught, by criticizing and refuting that which is given, we discover the paradoxical necessity of closing our eyes to what we can see so as to better understand the invisible forces driving the world around us. What a strange paradox: we need to close our eyes to see more clearly by gaining access to the world of abstraction. Children and young people enjoy discovering this way of thinking, the distancing of self from the environment in which we live. Many young ethnics are victims of isolation because they are unable to find a place for themselves in consumer society. And they don't have the means to *close their eyes* and distance themselves from themselves, to evaluate themselves, in other words to position themselves within the system where they are situated without being accepted. Borrowing from the ideas of Cornelius Castoriadis, we can say that self-extraction means standing on one's own shoulders and watching oneself looking toward the future.[2] It means asking: Who are you? What have you done? How long do you have left to live? With whom will you spend that time? It was a young ethnic who, during a debate about the importance of individual and social memory, shouted at me: "What's the point of memory when you don't have a future?" There I was telling my audience that you won't go far if you don't know where you're from, by which I meant that memory has exchange value in our encounters with the people we meet in the course of our lives. But he wanted to tell me that he had nothing with which to string together a future, for he had had a wretched start in life in the hood with an ethnic origin that brought him constant rejection. I immediately replied that it was precisely memory that made it possible to construct a future. I tried to explain that, to distance yourself from yourself, you have to learn the art of distance more generally, spatially and temporally. In terms of thought, this means learning to learn, observing a given object or situation from different angles, listening to the criticisms of others and benefiting from them.[3] I'm not sure whether the young man understood what I said, but, judging by the silence in the room, I think that those who were there had registered something that they would think about for a while. Something would be retained.

In many encounters I have noticed that, where distance is concerned, humor plays an important role in the analysis of intercultural relations. In the way that it plays on distances and transgresses frontiers, mockery can be comforting and convivial, a really effective social force. It is often said that, when someone doesn't have a sense of humor, that person is stuck, refusing to see any other point of view than his. A lack of humor is sometimes a sign of social poverty, reflecting a situation in which an individual cannot see beyond his immediate self. Let me give another striking example of this. I was in a hood giving a talk to a group of teenage interns in the course of which I was enthusing about great inventions and innovations in human history—Gutenberg, Vasco da Gama, Magellan, Pierre and Marie Curie—when a student raised his hand to ask a question. When I invited him to do so, he solemnly stated, without further ado, that he knew who had invented "le fil à couper le beurre" [the cheese wire or butter cutter]. That was all he had to say. Then he waited for me to ask him to say who it was. As the student was of Franco-French origin, I immediately scrutinized his face for a hint of some sort of joke based on a pun directed at me ("fil à couper le Beur"—Beur cutter!). Nothing. His expressionless face showed no sign of humor. So I went on: "The inventor of the Beur cutter? Oh, I know: It's Le Pen!" Without blinking, the young man looked at me in a completely detached way and then replied that that was, of course, not the inventor's name. I had been waiting for him to smile. But no. I thought perhaps he hadn't heard my reply. Then, with great authority, he quoted the name of Jean Somebody-or-Other who really had invented the butter thingamajig. He seemed pleased with what he'd said. Suddenly I found myself in the strange situation of trying to explain to this young man that *I had been joking*, that I had deliberately confused *le beurre* with *les Beurs* and that, as Le Pen was the enemy of the latter, *le fil à couper les Beurs* meant . . . But, the more I tried to explain all this, the more I saw the yawning chasm of incomprehension separating us. I had to resign myself to the fact that the young intern was unable to decode my joke on its second level. He understood the world on one simple level and only on that level, just like my father, who thought that the earth was flat and that the sun moved around it. It was, thus, clear that a pun, which necessarily disturbs the given order of things, was for some people as inaccessible as a complex mathematical equation because of the abstract processes of thought involved in it. Not everyone can handle such things. I never found out why the young man had mentioned the inventor of the butter cutter. Who knows—perhaps he had never even heard of the Beurs!

Didn't an astrophysicist friend once tell me that about one in three people in France still believe that the sun revolves around the earth? The figure seems quite credible to me.

I have often noted that, with young ethnics, humor and mockery don't go well with religious faith. There is no joking with God. On the contrary, he is to be feared because he is (the) Almighty. That doesn't prevent me from replying with veiled humor to all the students who ask me whether I am a Muslim that I practice religion but don't believe it. I like to turn things around, so, when people ask me why I practice religion without being a believer, I reply that it is by practicing faith that you can become a believer, as Pascal observed. When students press me to say what I think about religion, I say that faith is for me a private matter that concerns only God and me and that, when the final judgment comes, there will be no one between me and my conscience. Everyone agrees on that point. If a girl removes her Islamic head scarf before entering the schoolroom of the Republic, that does not in any way alter the relationship between her and God. The same goes for those who wear yarmulkes or Christian crosses.

We, Khaled Kelkal

Still with reference to God let me recall an important event in the history of the banlieues that took place in 1995. After a massive police manhunt a young presumed terrorist from the Lyon banlieue of Vaulx-en-Velin, Khaled Kelkal, was tracked down and shot dead in a blaze of publicity by paramilitary police in a wood on the outskirts of Lyon. His profile was not that of some ordinary terrorist, a dropout with no education and nothing to lose, like the young blacks in American ghettos described by James Baldwin. No, this young man, just twenty-two years old, had attended a junior high school in Vaulx-en-Velin and had then been a senior at a lycée not far from the primary school I had attended in the rue Sergent Blandan, where he had done quite well in chemistry. These aspects of his social trajectory seemed to be in complete contradiction with the Islamist terrorist he subsequently became. In contrast with the young intern who regarded the butter cutter as the invention of the century, Khaled Kelkal was able to read the world at several different levels, had personally experienced a certain amount of mobility, and had changed his *point of view* on a number of occasions. But this relatively wide field of experience did not prevent him from being brainwashed in prison. Shortly after his death *Le Monde* published a long interview that, by chance, a German researcher had conducted with Kelkal three years earlier.[4]

The interview provided extraordinary insights into the astonishing convictions on which the young man based his faith in Allah. Asked about the significance of Islam for him, Kelkal replied: "In truth, it means a huge amount to me. And I feel as if I'm still trying to grasp it all. I keep saying: 'I must be enveloped by religion. I must pray.' Every three or four days we rent a cassette [on which we see] authorities on Islam, and Westerners too, setting out the words of the Koran. A leading Japanese astronomer has certified that the Koran is the voice of God." After adding that "NASA's top scientist has also certified this," Kelkal concluded: "What is being said here [in the Koran] cannot be human. It must be divine. There is no denying it now. When top scientists certify it, it cannot be denied."

Here we see how far things can go when a young man forbids himself to deny or refute what Japanese and NASA scientists—people who explore the universe and can see it from above and afar—are supposed to have scientifically demonstrated: that the Koran is something true. In such circumstances the young man could not but accept such a "truth," just as my students did when I performed my sorcerologist's magic tricks.

Two factors seem to have contributed to Khaled Kelkal's psychological disorder. The first was his transfer from *collège* [junior high school] to lycée [senior high school]. His collège had been close to home, whereas the lycée was "far away," in downtown Lyon, in foreign territory, in another world. Moving there was an important reason for his saying: "I don't belong." In that downtown lycée he felt that he was no longer on his home territory, no longer among his friends, his own people.

He seems also to have been unable to resolve some

personal psychological problem that made it impossible for him to find a sense of belonging among unfamiliar people; in venturing outside the confines of Vaulx-en-Velin, he felt lost. One day, in prison, he met a Muslim chaplain who showed him another way, God's way, from which he had strayed. He jumped into it blindly with both feet. A similar psychological and political trajectory had been trodden by the African American leader Malcolm X in the 1970s, after his prison encounter with the leader of the Nation of Islam movement.[5] When you enter that kind of trajectory and close yourself off from other human beings, you become a bomb targeting democracy. Khaled Kelkal became consumed with the desire to destroy what he saw as rotten—a world that had failed to offer him a place—instead of asking himself whether he had really tried to find such a place with a sense of purpose and recognition.

When the distance between an individual and the rest of the world all but disappears, democracy is endangered. Objectivity disappears and, with it, lucidity. Others, people who are different, no longer exist. They become enemies or, at best, shadowy figures hovering on the edge of one's consciousness. The most violent and ultimate form of social exclusion is the *atomization* of the individual in a process that we can call *noyautage*, removing all the external layers that ordinarily link a person to the world outside. Stripped bare, the individual is unable to establish a distance between himself and others, unable to establish a sense of time and space, unable to mobilize any critical faculty, unable to say no. In a consumer society the propensity to ask questions becomes anesthetized; the superficial and the immediate replace depth and duration, and speed and impatience replace quiet reflection and perambulation. Thus, in the United States, for example, the war against Iraq in March 2003, falsely justified by the argument that weapons of mass destruction were threatening the democratic world, received overwhelming public support. At the height of the U.S.-led invasion it was difficult, if not dangerous, to express opposition to the war. At critical moments in the life of a nation it is as dangerous as it is easy to anesthetize critical faculties by appealing to the unreflecting core of the masses. We need to remember that, after the attacks of September 11, 2001, the nation's nerves were raw.

In France the banning of the Islamic head scarf in public schools touched a similar nerve in the identity of many young people of Maghrebi origin, among whom there is a widespread feeling of being deliberately refused recognition and excluded from the dominant system. This can lead them to seek solace in religion, which meets their need for bonds of spirituality, fraternity, and solidarity with a true family of people of their own kind. And perhaps we can see in this too a need to believe in a truly egalitarian society, one in which the dice are not loaded as they are beneath the surface of the Republic, where *birth* still plays a major role in distributing power among those who, in effect, inherit it. Islam is also a tool that can be used to inspire fear among the dominant population of the society into which young ethnics are born and of which they are legally citizens. Islam is the *quick-drying cement* of an identity that is widely visible in the media and well positioned to capitalize on the bitterness of those who have been disappointed by the republican myth of equality. The disappointment and disillusionment born of the unfulfilled promises of 1789 offer easy pickings to those who want to exploit them.

5

We Are Stronger Than *You*

Conspiracy theories. Paranoia. That is what binds together gangs of young ethnics within the confines of their neighborhoods. They construct and then feed the idea that the world outside is hostile and that teachers, policemen, firefighters, bus inspectors, judges, and, by extension, all those who wear a uniform are the official representatives of a world that is out to get them. By the same token within the gang the individual is supposed to find the solace of natural cohesion, of a shared predicament (that of the poor and the victimized, who become a family and a community), and of shared origins (which prompt the discrimination from which they suffer). The individual must give way to the codes and rules without which the community cannot maintain its cohesion. By the same token in such an environment a dérouilleur will find it hard to survive as an independent person. In Maghrebi families the most violent cultural break is that between an individual and his or her family, between *me* and *us*. This is also a struggle between *inside* and *outside*. It is tough for older brothers, for example, but it is even more difficult for girls, for whom the expression of their individuality often results in open conflict with the father, as Kalima, a woman doctor interviewed in the course of my research, explained:

> From the age of fifteen, sixteen, onward I knew it was bound to end in conflict because my parents' ideas made things impossible. When I was fifteen, the last thing I wanted was to get married and have children. A lot of girls in our situation feel the same way: they want to be recognized as individuals. My parents would always say: "*With us*, things are done this way or that"! For me, *with us* meant nothing; for me, what counted was not *with us* but *me*, the way *I* want to live. . . . The fact is I've always been very individualist. I think that's what saved me. If you're not individualist, within that kind of family you are swallowed up and never have a chance to blossom because you are constantly tortured by the desire not to hurt your parents. There comes a time when your individuality has to be recognized, when you feel the need to blossom as an individual. . . . At home I was always the one who refused to do as I was told. I told them I didn't want them to plan out my life for me, that I didn't want to be like that, and, as long as it was just a matter of words, it was OK because they simply didn't believe I was capable of doing what I said. But, although I loved my parents, I could manage without them, as I explained to them, because I had a job.

I worked to pay for my studies, so I was financially independent.[1]

Social emancipation comes through economic autonomy. When a young woman works and earns *her* own money, the way she is looked at depends on how she performs in that society, the status she attains in the world outside the family. For a dérouilleur, mobility brings new parameters of identification that permit his or her personality to develop far more readily than in the closed world of *within, with us*. To overcome the violent psychological barriers that you must inevitably confront, you must be very determined as an individual. For boys getting out almost inevitably means breaking with the kids you grew up with in the hood. When a dérouilleur has spent his teenage years with close friends in the hood, moving on is all the more difficult because it seems to mean leaving behind people you were once close to. The humorist Jamel Debbouze, brought up in the Paris banlieue of Trappes by Moroccan immigrant parents, has spoken about the concerns that are generated by success, including feelings of guilt toward the people you were once closest to.

Yet very few dérouilleurs regret the path that they have taken. Once you get out, you are glad to have found the personal distance you needed and to have escaped the smothering of your personality by the gang. You are glad to have escaped from the paranoia that flourishes in the self-enclosure of the group. When they achieve that personal distance, those who move on look askance at the inertia of those who are still rusting where they are and who are quick to present themselves as victims of society. One dérouilleur recounted that, when he returned to the hood after several years studying *abroad* (by which he meant the neighboring town!), he found several old friends who seemed literally *glued* to the neighborhood in which they had grown up. Twelve years on it was as if he had left them the previous day. After exchanging the usual courtesies about each other's health, they talked a little about soccer and about the past, and then their conversation dried up; they had nothing more to say to each other. There was simply nothing to talk about. Dérouilleurs and rouilleurs live in the same country but in different worlds. They no longer share a common spring from which to build a shared narrative.

Often rumors start to circulate about those who have succeeded outside, who in some cases are attacked by those who've stayed put. Violent rejection of this kind is often caused by jealousy. Dérouilleurs are, thus, perceived as doubly foreign: they are outsiders in the world they have newly entered, and they are no longer accepted where they came from. Getting a high-status job—this is especially true of those who have found places in local or national political institutions—makes them automatically suspect. This exclusion is hurtful to those concerned when they see themselves spat on by people from their own community because they have joined a political party; others are spurned as "French" because they have studied at a university, or as "whores" because they have decided to live away from their families, or as "Uncle Toms" because they work at city hall. Attacks of this kind against those who have entered public life or who have gone elsewhere to earn a living are commonplace. Fouad, for example, comments:

I lived entirely in Les Bosquets [in the northeastern banlieues of Paris] from 1986 to 1999. Since the fall of 1999

I've gone back there only on weekends. It's a very strange feeling because sometimes I feel as if I don't live there anymore while at other times it's as if I still live there because I go back every weekend to see my parents, my brothers and sisters and friends. . . . When I go back there, I feel excluded; some of my friends say I'm trying to lord it over them, giving myself airs and graces like I'm "French." I put up with what they say because I don't want any problems. I wish my family could get out of there. My buddies look at me askance when I go back. Personally I don't see how they can say I'm trying to build myself up as "French." All I want is a decent job. That's why I've been studying, and that's what I tell my buddies when they start getting at me: I'm doing what I'm doing *for me*. Later I'll be able to tell myself "you're where you wanted to be," and I won't owe anything to anyone else except for my family and myself. I try to explain this to some of the guys and tell them you have to think as an individual.[2]

Why are those who get out rejected in this way? One of the reasons is that those who succeed, those who gain personal autonomy, make brutally and unmistakably visible the immobility of those who rust where they are. Like reflecting mirrors, the liberation of some reinforces the feeling of imprisonment among others. That is why, when dérouilleurs return to the hood, they have to justify themselves. So they become the advocates of values such as effort, work, courage, solidarity, and respect for one's parents and for the individual. In so doing they become guides.

By attacking former members who have gone it alone, the gang tries to reassert its boundaries and reinforce its ramparts. Any personal, individual link with the world outside is regarded as an act of betrayal. Members of the group go "downtown" together, not on their own. They feel strength in numbers. And the dérouilleur who has gone over to the other camp is seen as impure—as an infidel—because of his contact with Others. It is not difficult to imagine the consequences of this kind of control over individual mobility when a young woman wants to leave this kind of group to marry a man from the other side!

The fact is that, within the hood, among the excluded, difference is rejected as violently as elsewhere. Whites are not the only victims of disjointed young ethnics. Their rejection of those who are different from them is not racially motivated. The victims of discrimination produce their own forms of exclusion, scapegoating those who get ahead through individual merit. Personal successes are regarded as suspect because, in the collective psyche of the minority, an individual possessing only his or her own personal talents can never succeed in mainstream society. If a guy succeeds, it's because he's become *a pig eater*, *a token Arab*, or a *bolo*. This last term entered public circulation after the violent disturbances that broke out during student demonstrations in Paris in March 2005:

> For students in a lycée where, according to the head teacher's estimate, 80 percent of the students are young people "of color," everything pointed toward "*petits blancs*" *parisiens* [white working-class Parisians] as ideal victims. In their slang those victims are called *bolos* (or sometimes *borros*). "A bolo is a sucker, a victim," explains Heikel, though he, like his classmates, is unable to explain the origin of the word. "It's as if 'come and steal my stuff' was

written across their faces," says nineteen-year-old Patty, a resident of Sevran, who was not present during the demonstrations and who was critical of the violence. "Bolos look down because they're afraid, because they're cowards," says another nineteen-year-old high school student in the second year of the Brevet d'Etudes Profesionnelles [BEP—vocational certificate] program. "A Maghrebi can be a bolo if he thinks like a French person," adds Rachid, from Montreuil. "If he talks with his sister about sex, for example."[3]

For a dérouilleur there is a great risk of being regarded by rouilleurs as someone who has taken on the mentality of the French, simply because he has gone to live on the other side of the barrier. He will try in vain to get them to understand that, if he's succeeded, it's because he made certain choices, learned certain skills, and worked hard to get *where he wanted to be*, as Fouad would put it. Yet the truth is that the world on the other side of the tracks is not governed by a pure and perfect system of competition with fair treatment for everyone, including young ethnics. They have found jobs in certain professions *because that is where they are wanted*. There is, thus, considerable ambiguity concerning the extent to which the *origins* of candidates are taken into account in recruitment procedures. For instance, when it comes to political positions, the choice of candidates is often affected by their territorial origins (the banlieues) or ethnic origins (having immigrant parents), and this clouds the standing of people who want to be seen as holding office solely on the basis of their personal merit. Political parties have an interest in making ethnically marked candidates visible in order to display their modernity and their commitment to diversity, especially with an eye on young voters. Paradoxically, in elections to regional councils, the Front National was ahead of other parties in 1998 in securing the election of four candidates of Maghrebi origin in the Ile-de-France (Greater Paris) and Provence-Alpes-Côte-d'Azur regions. The Front National leader, Jean-Marie Le Pen, regularly defends himself against accusations of racism by citing the way he has enabled candidates of Maghrebi origin to get elected, in contrast with other politicians, who talk about doing this but do not actually put it into practice. The naming of their origins constantly complicates the public standing of those who gain elected offices. Thus, a *dérouilleur* who accedes to public office is apt to receive requests from coethnics appealing to a sense of ethnic solidarity, people whom he has to keep at arm's length (through a kind of ethnic distance) because he has to maintain neutrality (technical distance) in order to be regarded as legitimate by majority ethnics.[4] He finds himself trapped in a paradoxical bind that blurs the distinction between his private and public lives. When he attains a position of power, he is seen as *one of us, someone from our side* who has broken through into the other camp, someone to whom it is natural to address ethnically based requests, solicitations for mutual back-scratching and special favors—on the assumption that all societies work that way. As a result someone *from our side* who doesn't play the game as expected when he gets into a position of power is felt to be penalizing his own people. It is assumed that corrupt systems all work the same way: if you don't play the game the way it is, you are discriminated against and out of the running right from the start; there is no point competing because you've lost before you even start.

To take an analogy from the field of professional sport, when a debate was raging in the media a few years ago about the use of performance-enhancing drugs, the argument was made that an athlete who didn't take drugs had no chance of winning. Similar ideas exist in an unequal society in which the weak believe that everything is rigged against them and that the strong remain strong because they cheat. In this view of things the wider world beyond that of our camp is seen as a lawless jungle in which violence and vice reign supreme. It is the world of *Dallas*, the 1980s American television series. It is a world that knows no pity. From this springs the idea that those in power—or, in a more general sense, "the system"—have invented the myth of equal opportunities to strengthen their domination over the weak. And, when an individual, a dérouilleur, decides to go it alone and leave the pack behind, this is interpreted as proof of a conspiracy. He becomes the *tree concealing the forest*. If you believe in conspiracy theory it is natural to turn to your community of origin, especially when it has a religious dimension, as a political resource.

Islam Outweighs Citizenship

In stark contrast to their parents, postwar immigrant workers ignored by the host society, from which they often kept their distance in anticipation of eventually returning to their home country, the children of those immigrants made their social presence highly visible during the 1980s. In 1983 the first nationwide demonstration by second-generation Maghrebis, which the media called the March of the Beurs, became a multicolored, joyful, and triumphant reference point showing young ethnics that the way to gain social dignity was through collective action, by going out into the rue de la République and occupying it. This was a turning point in the history of multicultural France, giving rise to the notion that, if you want to count politically, you must make yourself visible and count your numbers. This was when the Beurs really began to show how rooted they were in France. Paradoxically this was also when the myth of republican egalitarianism began to become tarnished. The appeal to numbers, to a community of one's own kind, was used as a tool in what one might ironically call a kind of *ethnic trade unionism*. To make your voice heard you had to carry electoral weight, for elections were the place in which you acquired legitimacy within the Republic. Quantitative demographic arguments thus became strategies for occupying public space. Out of that first collective experience came the slogan ten years later: "Five or six million Muslims in France count!" This slogan is not without confusion, for it misleadingly amalgamates numerous individuals under the label *Muslim* when there are, in reality, many differences among them. But this did not prevent the slogan from being heard at the headquarters of political parties. Its resonance tells us a lot, more generally, about a change in the way politics works and in the way citizens seek to use the services of their elected representatives. A generation ago, on a given day each week a député would meet with constituents who had requested appointments as individuals. Theirs was a one-on-one dialogue in which the constituent would ask for help, a personal favor, or a job with the city council. Today things have changed. Now citizens go to see their député as part of a group, carrying petitions, and threaten that, if they do not receive quick responses to their complaints, they will turn to the député's political opponent. A one-on-one relationship has been replaced by forms of group pressure based on ethnic factionalism. Like other citizens groups of Muslims in the hoods have understood this change in the relation between political supply and demand. By capitalizing on the frustrated aspirations of many young ethnics who feel cheated by party politics and social injustices, they strike a chord in the electoral marketplace. In the final analysis it is not so much young ethnics or Muslims who have factionalized the Republic; rather, they have simply followed the logic of the way in which *the electoral market* has developed. The principle of republican individualism, "one man, one vote," has been replaced by "recognition for each community," a modus operandi on which politicians and religious leaders now seem to agree. If, in an electoral constituency, an ethnic community brandishes its voting power in support of particular demands, the local mayor or député is faced with a very difficult dilemma. Often he will claim that a *community of electors* is not really an ethnic community but simply a neutral aggregate of electors with whom it is necessary to engage. They call it *political realism*. In so doing they hypocritically ratchet the wheel one turn further.

If France had seized the opportunity that was there in the 1980s, a less demagogic path could have been taken. But the opportunity was lost. In response to each banlieue revolt successive governments reacted in lukewarm or Machiavellian fashion, brandishing and gradually devaluing the words *equality, fraternity, solidarity*, and *citizenship*. Worse still, whenever young ethnics attempted to improve their lot through collective action within the republican framework, they were rebutted by a tired conservative discourse warning of the floodgates that were in danger of being opened to other minority groups—homosexuals, Corsicans, the handicapped, the short, the tall, etc., etc.—and assaulted with a word that, through misuse, also lost its power: *communautarisme* [ethnic separatism or factionalism]. The truth is that there are many different forms of *communautarisme*. How can anyone hope to conceal from young ethnics in the hoods that forms of preferential treatment abound in our society, from the institutions of social reproduction that are the *grandes écoles* [elite institutions of higher education] to other *communities of people of the same kind*—political parties and networks or clubs, trade unions, sects, etc.—that are undoubtedly at work in society, skewing its theoretical equality of opportunities? How can anyone conceal from young ethnics the fact that, unlike our Anglo-Saxon neighbors, France with its five or six million people of Arabo-Islamic heritage does not have a single elected member of parliament originating in that part of the national population? In many towns containing ethnicized hoods in which whites are a numerical minority, there is not a single city council member of color. The Left carries a heavy historical responsibility for this, and that responsibility will continue to weigh on it. It instrumentalized the question of the banlieues in its political battle with the Right, stifling the Beurs' desire for political emancipation by backing sos-Racisme, which, in 1985, snatched out of the hands of the young activists from Les Minguettes in Vénissieux the political momentum with which, two years earlier, they had launched the Marche des Beurs. When, in 2002, Jacques Chirac appointed to the center-right government two junior members of Maghrebi origin, the Socialist Party brazenly attempted to outscore him at its congress in Dijon in May 2003 by committing the party to ensure that 15–20 percent of its national officials would, henceforth, be of foreign origin. Among them was the third president of sos-Racisme, Malek Boutih, of Algerian origin. When the party instituted this brazen and arbitrary *quota*, it did not stir so much as a murmur in French political circles. Was there a feeling that it was better late than never? Not necessarily. In the hoods the *huge scam* that the Socialists had perpetrated earlier had left a deep imprint on collective memories. Maybe the Right would follow through with its new momentum? Alas, no. The 2004 elections brought further disillusionment to young ethnics, for all those who had hoped for winnable positions on the lists of candidates for departmental and regional councils fielded by the Right were disappointed.

Those elections illustrated yet again how, during an entire generation, political parties have been playing young ethnics like a yo-yo. When it comes to sharing power, when integration becomes a zero-sum game, the stakes become so high that vague multicultural sentiments count for nothing in the face of personal ambitions. All this plays into the hands of ethnic factionalists out to make hay in the hoods, sneering at the myths of republican equality and the illusory promises of individual success.

So what is to be done? Shall we let the Republic slide down the slippery slope of least resistance, succumbing to the law of the strongest, the richest, the most influential, or shall we renew the fight to give a real chance to democracy, individual merit, and social blending? It is in the second direction that republicans committed to seizing this last chance see the future of France in all its diversity. We must engage in this direction without hypocrisy or naïveté, no longer on the basis of a republication *pact*, but this time on the basis of a republican *contract* with real guarantees for those still willing to trust the system to deliver a fair place to them. And this time it means taking the elevator, not the stairs.

6   Equal Opportunities

Beyond Integration

If we look back on the last quarter of a century in the banlieues, we can see that Muslim girls have been by no means the only ones covering their faces. A quarter century of political neglect has spawned and nourished feelings of ethnic solidarity and factionalism among those excluded by virtue of the color of their face. There is now an entire generation for whom the word *integration* evokes ambiguity, trickery, and disillusionment. The word now crackles provocatively and aggressively in the ears of young ethnics. *Integrated*? They already are! They are part of French society. They were born into it! They are French *by birth* but *not recognized* as such.

Integration? The word has wilted and lost its power. Canny politicians aware of what is happening on the ground know that it is now unwise to use that word when talking to young ethnics, for it simply arouses their ire. Others, less well-informed, continue to use the word in the vain hope of disguising their ignorance and insensitivity. *Integration.* The word is now anachronistic in relation to the agenda of today's young ethnics, for whom the issue is social recognition. That is why we should now make every effort to avoid the word so that we can rid ourselves of all the out-of-date ideas that go with it. Dropping the word forces us to change our *point of view* and see things from a new angle, one in which the real issues are the manifest presence of young ethnics in France and the need to crack down on the discrimination from which they suffer. For an entire generation the rhetoric of integration has de facto held them on a horizontal social plane. The time has come to move to a vertical plane. The image of a social elevator corresponds most closely to the new direction in which France must now head. Vertical mobility is what we now need if we are to make manifest the multicolored, multicultural France that until now has been seen only in our soccer and other athletic stadiums. Away with integration. We urgently need to invent a new and more modern notion of social recognition, new forms of participatory democracy, and new citizen-ambassadors for equal opportunities. The word *mobility* best corresponds to the new outlook that France needs if it is to save what is left of 1789.

The Future Starts Here

The time for moving like crabs has gone! Migrant families have long since moved on from the myth of a return to the homeland that in days gone by hampered their settlement in France. Those families now accept that the future of their children is *here*, not *over there*. The dream of *over there* was a past that we might say, in the spirit of Auguste Comte, silently shaped the future. This shift means that young people of foreign origin are now definitively rooted in the land of their birth and that, among these populations, there is now a demand for a real future here, especially for the younger generation. We can see this in the fields of public and even private education, in matters such as law and order and the environment, in other words in demands for public services similar to those of the majority ethnic population. A major symbolic turning point in building the French melting pot piece by piece lies in the access of young ethnics to the nation's police forces. The time is ripe for young ethnics to gain social legitimacy by entering those police forces. This is a key social goal. When the recruitment of young ethnics into the police forces becomes an ordinary event, information about and investment in public services will spread throughout the hoods, along with respect for uniforms and a general acceptance of the police. When you are arrested by an officer of the law and the color of his skin no longer matters, things will no longer be the same.

Significantly, if we look at the way in which jobs in the security industry have developed in the last few years in department stores and banks, we can see that those jobs have become very accessible to Beurs and blacks, as, indeed, have jobs as racial profilers and bouncers at discotheques. Beurs and blacks doing those jobs are generally respected by young ethnics even when their orders are to keep them out. Although their exclusion is even more pernicious in such circumstances—since those keeping them out are of their own kind—we see no acts of collective violence against these ethnic filters.

There is also another factor generating demands for better security among minorities as among the rest of the population. This concerns the steady weakening of conventional forms of ethnic belonging among young ethnics despite huge media coverage of the alleged growth of Islam in the hoods and the efforts of those who try to exploit this. The shift from the *dérouilleurs* of the 1970s and 1980s to the *sauvageons* [wild children or young savages] of the 1990s and beyond goes hand in hand with a shift from the social fabric of the village to the more complex social relations of the city.[1] There has been an identity shift between yesterday's grands frères and today's young ethnics, who identify far less with the ethnic origins of their immigrant forebears and are far less preoccupied with the legacy of the colonial period. They know less and less about the history of immigration in France and overseas colonization. Their relation with the past, their sense of long-term duration and depth, has been overtaken by a preoccupation with the present, with the superficial, and with instant gratification. Today the identity of these youths is shaped instinctively by a shared sense of belonging to a particular place and age group rather than by shared ethnic origins. This is apparent in the gangs we see in the hoods. For example, during a spectacular clash between gangs from rival hoods that took place in the Paris business district of La Défense early in 2001, I remember being struck by the way a young ethnic indignantly told reporters that he had been there purely by chance and had been among those attacked despite the fact that he was of Maghrebi origin! He had learned to his cost that his swarthy skin no longer served as a guarantee of tacit belonging to a particular tribe able to protect him from attack. Other criteria had emerged in the look of the Other, such as that of being on friendly or enemy territory. There was another example of this during the attacks on high school demonstrators in March 2005, which generated much talk about the phenomenon of "gutting [robbing] people" when young petits blancs were attacked and robbed of their cell phones, MP3 players, and other articles of value. People wanted to know whether petits blancs had been the sole targets of these attacks. To find out more about this a meeting with young blacks was organized by a youth worker in Grigny, a banlieue in the *département* of Essonne, in the presence of a journalist. When asked if "a black with the same external signs of wealth as a white could be 'gutted,'" a youth called Rudy replied: "It depends on whether he's from the same town or the same hood. If he's from Evry and he comes up against some guys from Grigny, they could gut him." Another youth added: "It's just the same as attacking a weak white. Guys will attack a hood that they don't think will carry out reprisals."[2]

These remarks, taken almost at random from recent events, confirm the steady erosion of conventional forms of ethnic belonging to which I have already referred among young ethnics. These examples can readily be compared with similar phenomena in poor neighborhoods of Los Angeles, where there is a long-established pattern of gangs building territorial identities that far outweigh any other form of belonging. One of the reasons for the steady decline in ethnic in favor of territorial references lies in what we can call the *hollowing out* of these youths. Socially they no longer feel multiple allegiances. The core of their identity has been reduced to the fusion of their personality with a place (the hood, the tower block, the entrance to their apartment complex, etc.). Different generations are no longer bound together. Ignorance and forgetfulness have done their work. These youths have been, so to speak, gutted of any feelings of family, social, or cultural solidarity and transformed into mere consumers.

It should be added that the growing isolation of individuals within modern cities is partly a result of the growing complexity of social relations. With each passing year the hoods in the banlieues have taken in poor folks who are increasingly disparate in their cultural origins and history, thereby weakening the basis for constructing a shared social fabric. In the absence of a shared history it has become practically impossible to construct a sense of social cohesion.

It is in these difficult circumstances that *ethnic policemen* make their appearance in urban spaces. As was the case with the pieds-noirs when they arrived in France, police forces, fire departments, and the security industry in general are potentially important sources of jobs for young ethnics, who by the same token are liable to become increasingly important guarantors of social cohesion, provided that they believe in the principle of equal opportunities.

Whaddaya Mean, Equal Opportunities?

The principle of equal opportunities is based on a liberal form of social organization that rests on three main pillars: *individualism*, which accords primacy to the individual over the group of which he or she is a member; *meritocracy*, which valorizes individual merit and talent in the competition for social goods; and *universalism*, according to which all individuals competing for such goods receive equal treatment. Although there is a wide consensus in Western countries in favor of the principle of equal opportunities, there are many differences concerning its implementation.

The Idea of Equal Opportunities

The idea of equal opportunities is often compared with that of a race in which the best runner wins. For this to work the race has to be organized in such a way as to ensure that it takes place fairly, giving each participant an equal chance to prove his or her merit. If we compare the competition for entry to a grande école with a race, those who are granted entry are those who demonstrate the greatest ability, measured on a common scale for all applicants. When a job is offered, the person appointed will in principle be the one who looks the strongest in terms of qualifications, skills, experience, etc. The exact antithesis of a discriminatory approach, a policy of equal opportunities must guarantee that it is always the most meritworthy person that wins.

The race is run between the starting blocks at one end and the finish line at the other. If all the candidates for a given job set off simultaneously from the same starting point, the competition serves to separate them before they reach the finish line. In theory, within this model of pure and perfect social competition, analogous to the axioms that informed neoclassical economic thinking, nothing should interfere with the link between personal merit and the finishing order of the competitors. In theory, all the job candidates set out on an equal footing from the same starting blocks. But, in practice, this isn't true, for at least three reasons.

The first reason concerns the relationship between the starting line and social distinctions, as theorized by Pierre Bourdieu.[3] It flies in the face of the truth to say that all those individuals at the starting blocks, ready to set out on the race, do so from a position of equality. An ahistorical egalitarian model ignores the different social histories of competitors, notably where their cultural baggage is concerned. In such a model that baggage is empty, containing neither memory nor experience. In reality the race is skewed from the outset by the differential nature of social reproduction, in which older generations of the "meritorious" pass on the baton to their descendants in the competition for jobs. There is no need to belabor the point that, in the national education system, the chances of success of children of well-off parents are vastly higher than are the chances of children from low-income families.[4]

ACCESS TO INFORMATION

The second problem with the pure competition model concerns the identity of the candidates setting out from the starting line: Who are they, and how representative are they of society as a whole? This raises the question of differential access to information. Does every individual know that the competition exists and how it operates? Manifestly, no. Depending on their particular social histories, class background, and other social networks, citizens have *different* degrees of access to information and, in some cases, no access to information at all. Sometimes they may even be given false information. It follows from this that a process of selection takes place *before* the starting line, for the candidates ready to start the race are those who knew the paths, modes of access, and rules by which to reach that position. Knowledge of that kind is not given to any and every ordinary person.

So what should be done about those outside key forms of information flow? What should we do about the young ethnics who, unconsciously or by some internalized form of stigmatization, rule out of their thinking from the outset any notion of competing for access to the grandes écoles, to high social offices, or to the ranks of the police forces? Should we stand fast on the original principle, insisting that they learn and apply the same rules as everyone else, meaning that it is up to them to "go and find the information the same as everyone else" in a logic of pure *egalitarianism*, or should we try to devise new ways of bringing the information to them in their outlying, marginalized spaces, in a logic of *equalization*?

Asking this question opens up a new way of implementing equal opportunities that we can call *irrigation*, the idea of which is to bring to the starting line a pool of candidates representative of the diversity within our society by targeting individuals outside ordinary information flows. This has nothing to do with the charitable idea of *la discrimination positive* [positive discrimination], the French expression for what is known in the United States as *affirmative action*. Instead the idea is to put in place ahead of the starting line ways of equalizing access to information about social mobility. As in a telecommunications system, it means putting into place relay or booster stations.

WHO REFEREES THE RACE?

To complete our sports analogy we need to consider a third flaw in the myth of equal opportunities, a flaw that, in this case, has to do with the organization of the race itself. It is often said that "we are all human," especially when someone in a position of authority makes a mistake. In the same way we can say that "equality of opportunity is human," meaning that, when implemented, such a notion can reproduce structural inequalities in a society and even contain hidden discriminatory practices. In France recruiters have long engaged openly or secretly in discriminatory practices that have nothing to do with judging the skills, merits, or strengths of individual candidates. Such practices are now public knowledge, following considerable media exposure. The rejection of candidates on the vague pretext that they are not the "right type" has meant the denial of jobs to many young ethnics, who have found it extremely difficult to prove in a way that will hold up in court that they are the victims of discrimination. Racial or ethnic discrimination of this kind has been rife in France for at least thirty years. Among young ethnics in the hoods victimized in this way it has generated a deep-seated culture of distrust and, sometimes, of outright rejection and defiance of republican myths. It follows from this that we need newly legitimated referees if we are to restore credibility in the idea of equal opportunities as a fair race open to all.

Against Their Will

Most European countries have laws prohibiting discrimination against individuals associated with ethnic groups seen as illegitimate or unacceptably foreign by members of the dominant population. Those laws are seldom very effective. They generally outlaw direct, explicitly racial discrimination but do little to combat indirect forms of discrimination, which are often institutional in nature.

These were codified in the European Union's 2000 directive on combating racial discrimination. Equal opportunities are subverted in numerous ways, such as "internal" appointments, those made via word of mouth or on the basis of personal recommendations, meaning that selections are made on the basis of criteria that preempt a genuinely open competition. Sometimes jobs are advertised with requirements that bear no relation to the work needing to be done and that have the effect of immediately ruling out many young ethnics. Such requirements can take the form of a graduate degree in a foreign language, effectively ruling out many youths in the hoods, or a university degree as well as a high school diploma for unskilled jobs, again ruling out many potential applicants, or the prohibition of certain forms of dress unconnected with the necessary job skills.

Public intervention is necessary in order to fight this very real *inequality of opportunity*, which in France often affects Maghrebis and blacks more severely than anyone else. For it is they who are the most widely affected by racial discrimination. This is the case, for example, in retailing, where employers often cite the supposed impact on customer relations.[5] Similar forms of discrimination are also present in numerous other aspects of daily life.

Trying to correct the differential situations created by discrimination can create further problems. Certain measures designed to reduce handicaps accumulated by a minority group in the past can, if applied to an individual without regard for his or her personal merit, create new individual injustices. It is, therefore, essential to distinguish between individuals and the groups in which they originate. Not all individuals originating in a minority suffering from discrimination are necessarily victims of that discrimination. For example, among Maghrebis light-skinned Kabyles can escape anti-Arab racism.[6] It is also the case that not every member of the dominant group has a privileged status. In other words, *while the supposed belonging of an individual to a given minority group is often the sole reason for discriminating against him or her, action in favor of the social promotion of an individual can never be justified solely on the basis of his or her claim to be a member of such a group.* Young ethnics might understandably feel that this double bind is unjust and injurious to them, but, if we are looking for effective solutions to inequality, we must accept this and move forward accordingly. We need to make clear our opposition to any policy that would favor the social promotion of an individual simply because he or she bears exterior signs of belonging to a community suffering from discrimination. The *French blender* cannot do its work on the basis of a rigid system imposing mandatory *quotas* with fixed percentages. It will take years of commitment and eternal vigilance to secure that blending. Realizing this, I am all the more disappointed personally by the extraordinary slowness of the system during an entire generation in responding to the urgent demands of young ethnics for proper social recognition. Overconfidence in the so-called French model of integration prevented those in power from seeing what might usefully have been borrowed from the experiences of the British, the Americans, the Canadians, the Dutch, and the Belgians. This blindness has greatly damaged French universalism.

Thirsty for Practical Action
I have already underscored the reality that most young ethnics feel violently frustrated by the way they are

spurned by mainstream society. Many envy the benefits gained in the United States since the 1960s through the civil rights movement. It is no accident if, in the United States, public policy has moved vigorously and pragmatically to rectify inequalities suffered by ethnic minorities. The history of the United States is built on centuries of institutional discrimination, initially through slavery, and then through segregation, which continued until the middle of the twentieth century. To remedy this racist past a range of measures—some of which were referred to as *affirmative action*—were brought to bear on the problem of segregation in the 1960s. Since then, U.S. policy in this field has gone through three main phases, the study of which offers useful lessons for the situation in France.

In the codification of U.S. antidiscrimination policy the phrase *affirmative action* first appeared in the Civil Rights Act of 1964 and then in a 1965 executive order on the implementation of that law in the field of employment. At no point in this first phase was there any question of building a system of "positive" or "reverse" discrimination granting preferential treatment to individuals on the basis of racial or ethnic origins irrespective of their talents, skills, or qualifications. Affirmative action has been misrepresented in this respect so often in France by those opposed to any attempt at rectifying inequalities that this point needs to be underscored. The 1964 law called for *concrete action*—that was the real sense of *affirmative action*—in two main respects: increased awareness on the part of employers of the importance of equal opportunities and concrete forms of assistance to minority ethnic groups officially recognized as having suffered from a long history of discrimination, as was the case with blacks, Native Americans, Hispanics, and certain Asian groups.

The most obvious sign of the handicaps accumulated by these groups lay in their relatively low levels of educational attainment and formal qualifications. To remedy this situation the law allowed special training programs to be established to enable minorities to acquire the necessary knowledge and skills to overcome such obstacles to social mobility. If we return to our analogy of the race, training programs of this kind went purposefully in search of victims of discrimination in order to pull them up to a fair position on the starting line with a genuinely equal opportunity to compete against other candidates in the job market. Companies were asked to take active and effective measures to ensure equality of opportunity by adopting recruitment and promotion procedures giving due weight to ethnic factors, as in the diversity charter recommended in France by the Institut Montaigne in 2004.[7] In line with this a system of ethnic monitoring was instituted in the United States and elsewhere, measuring the proportion of different ethnic groups among job candidates and those appointed and promoted by employers. If equality of opportunity is genuinely operational, policies of this kind should result in a situation in which the various ethnic groups are represented at all corporate levels in proportions that broadly reflect their proportions in the general population. If France is to ensure genuine equality of opportunity, special programs such as those that have long existed in the United States must be implemented so as to enable everyone to put themselves forward as well as possible.

*When You're Good, You're Good; When You're Something
Else, You're Something Else*

In the United States this approach changed in the second phase of affirmative action. In the 1970s a number of federal court rulings and instructions issued by the Equal Employment Opportunity Commission (EEOC), responsible for enforcing antidiscrimination policy in the field of employment, opened the way for fixed ethnic quotas irrespective of the skills or qualifications of individuals. This shift sometimes occurred incrementally in response to court or EEOC rulings instructing companies to achieve certain targets within set time frames. The effect was that, as the deadline approached, if a company had not attained the target by recruiting from ethnic minorities solely on the basis of merit, ethnic criteria would be given priority in order to meet the target. In this way a policy designed to ensure equality of opportunity led to the sorry pass in which companies applied crude ethnic quotas, thereby denying jobs to members of the majority ethnic group purely on the basis of their ethnicity.

Diversity, Quality, and Quantity

In France it was Nicolas Sarkozy who, in 2003, stirred things up when, without fully thinking things through, he launched a public debate on "positive discrimination" with the aim of giving new momentum to our democracy. Alas, things went badly wrong when he called for the appointment of a "Muslim prefect," immediately vaporizing any possibility of public opinion following his lead. Using a religious label—and a label evoking not just any religion but Islam, which has by no means the most positive reputation among the majority ethnic population!—and applying it to a policy that was supposedly designed to redress social inequalities in our country was the surest way of signaling to the French that Arabs, Muslims, and immigrants were to be given priority on the grounds that they were the victims of history, of racism, and of other forms of discrimination.[8] Talking about a "Muslim prefect" was the key mistake not to make if conservative republicans in France were to be convinced of the urgency of *making a reality* of multicolored France instead of simply talking about it. The confusion resulting from this made it quite impossible to convey the real message. M. Sarkozy tried in vain to correct his unfortunate choice of words by saying that he had meant to say "a prefect from a Muslim background"; he had committed a major political error by giving ready-made ammunition to opponents of any effective policy aimed at ensuring equality of opportunity. Is it possible that he pronounced the words *Muslim prefect* spontaneously and without self-control? Can a minister of that stature, one who, we are told, dreams while shaving every morning of being president of France in 2007, ask us to believe that he makes unpremeditated public declarations? I don't think so. In any event the effect of his statement on public opinion was unmistakable. It was in vain that M. Sarkozy would later say that Aïssa Dermouche was above all an internationally renowned economist and the director of the Nantes Business School, highlighting his professional talents and achievements instead of his supposed religion; the die had been cast—and loaded. The new prefect, M. Dermouche, had been turned into a Muslim, forcibly converted, as it were, by a supposedly secular minister of the French Republic.

Was M. Sarkozy afraid of pronouncing the word

Arab? Did it seem too stained in his mind and in that of public opinion, as it did for the radio listener to whom I referred earlier in this book?[9] Did he not dare to say *Français d'origine maghrébine* [French of Maghrebi origin] because that expression was more associated with youths in the hoods and could not, therefore, be applied to an economics professor and business school director? That too is possible. However it may be, one cannot but be astonished by such a serious political error on the part of a man who is himself the son of a Hungarian immigrant, who, at the relatively young age of fifty, had no personal memory of the Algerian war, and who consequently was not conditioned to think of Algerians in terms of labels current during the colonial period such as *Muslims, natives*, or even *Mohammedans*. It was perfectly open to him to speak simply of the appointment of a prefect of Maghrebi immigrant origin, which would have been perfectly accurate and far less loaded.

This was not the first time that a minister in the government of Jean-Pierre Raffarin got into a tangle with impromptu name-calling in reference to French citizens of Maghrebi origin.[10] The government spokesman Jean-François Copé, at that time even younger than M. Sarkozy, also referred to the junior ministers Hamlaoui Mékachéra and Tokia Saïfi by their supposed religious affiliation. This occurred on November 26, 2002, during a debate in the National Assembly on a constitutional proposal put forward by Socialist députés in favor of granting voting rights to foreigners. After four hours of rowdy debate the proposal was rejected by the assembly's right-of-center majority. It was in this context that the same Jean-François Copé, the official government spokesman, explained that the proposal was unacceptable because it broke the link between nationality and citizenship. "The real issue," he said, "is successful integration." He then provoked outrage among députés on the Left when, responding to the debate, he expressed delight at the fact that, for the first time, the government included two Muslim ministers. Denouncing what he called a "gaffe" revealing the "deeply reactionary" nature of the Right, the president of the Socialist Group had the session suspended. Then Copé tried to "dispel the misunderstanding" by referring to the "superb path of integration" trodden by the ministers concerned. There could scarcely be a clearer illustration of the confused thinking surrounding the population of North African immigrant origin, even at the highest levels of state.[11] The point is all the more pertinent in the National Assembly, where there is not a single député of that origin.

If we want to talk about "them," how can this be done if not by referring to "their" ethnic origins or the region in which "they" originate? This takes us to the heart of the problem: How are we to talk of the Others who are there, all around us, yet not in among us or part of us? These semantic issues point to the paradoxical nature of a relationship that is at the same time one of proximity and distance. Fifty years after the first wave of Maghrebi immigrant settlement in France the transplant is still being rejected. One of the reasons for this is that French society is still haunted by the ghosts of the colonial period.[12] The ghost of Sergeant Blandan, who left Lyon for the Algerian city of Bône on September 9, 1837, to take part in the fighting in the province of Constantine against the Harachtas, against Ahmed the former bey of Constantine, and the tribe of Oued Radjett, is still a living memory. The effects of the violence committed during the wars waged in the course of modern French history, notably in Algeria, cling all the more to that history to the extent that they are denied. We need the lid to be pulled off this history.[13]

Though born in *metropolitan* France, the children of immigrants are still seen as the children of colonial subjects, as the descendants of "natives" and "Muslims." They are still the "they" whom "we" (Gauls? descendants of Vercingetorix? Merovingians?) have honored by accepting them into our "host society." In 2004 ministers of the French Republic still instinctively call them *Muslims*, just as their parents and grandparents did in colonial North Africa. Today policies on urban issues, integration, equal opportunities, and law and order are all impregnated by the legacy of colonialism. Anti-Arab racism is often grounded in rancorous sentiments that say: "You kicked us out of Algeria in 1962; you're not going to take over here now!" Against this historical background, in calling for the appointment of a "Muslim prefect" Nicolas Sarkozy simply reinforced in the collective imagination of the dominant population the idea that, after stealing the jobs and livelihoods of the French, "Muslims/Arabs/natives" are now set to become the profiteers of positive discrimination policies. Conspiracy theories thus abound on both sides.

It is, therefore, best to expunge from our vocabulary not only *integration* but also *positive discrimination*, which is open to misunderstanding, suggesting conflict between majority and minority ethnic groups. I regret this, for, since the late 1980s, when I first went to the United States as a visiting professor at Cornell University, I have been fascinated by the pragmatic way in which different ethnic groups have been mixed together in that enormous country. I was struck the most by what I saw on television. Journalists of every color under the sun held front-rank positions in prime-time slots. So ethnic mixing was possible. And, the more they were mixed by ethnicity or gender, the less attention you paid to the origins of the TV presenters, and the more you listened to what they had to say and why they were there: the news!

Why didn't we see anything comparable to that in France? I wondered enviously. What needed to be done to make multicolored TV a reality in my country? After fifteen years in my ZUP in the La Duchère hood of Lyon, I was fascinated by the country of Martin Luther King. I was one of the first Beurs, born in a French shantytown, to be invited to a prestigious American university, from which I returned to France convinced that my country could not afford to pass up the benefits of affirmative action. In my work as a researcher with the CNRS, I became in the early 1990s a pioneer for positive discrimination in France. The only problem was that, in the United States, it was commonplace to speak of *ethnic minorities*, whereas, in France, this phrase was held to be devoid of meaning. In my country only citizens were recognized, and, since 1789, those free citizens were supposed to have been immune from discrimination on account of their origins. During that period I constantly returned to this theme in my public statements, to the point where I became nicknamed "the champion of positive discrimination":

> During the last few years, Azouz Begag has been fighting for "positive discrimination," for the idea of every public service earmarking a number of positions for French citizens of immigrant origin. In his view, this is the only effective tool against the *ethno-communautarisme* [ethnic

factionalism] that he says is "threatening our Republic." "Everybody can see this, but no one is doing anything about it," he says. His fear is that young people of immigrant origin could end up hardening their positions "in the way the Black Panthers did."[14]

That was what I said ten years ago. Time has proved me right.

Today, if we want to save what we can of the spirit of 1789, we need to approach equal opportunities from a different angle, such as that in which the Institut d'Etudes Politiques de Paris, popularly known as Sciences Po, has been engaged during the last few years. An additional entry channel to this top-ranking political science institute has been established for high-flying students from lycées in disadvantaged urban areas. Because this works on a spatially defined basis, no one is hurt on account of his or her ethnicity, which is important for the political viability of this approach.

Today France needs a blender with *differential tuning* of the principle of equal opportunities. As this is a sensitive field for the Republic, we must be careful to promote equal opportunities in a way that carries public opinion with us. The point can be illustrated by an analogy with a component in the axles of a car known as the differential. This is a mechanical system invented to ensure that, when a car goes round a bend, it remains properly balanced despite the fact that, during the turn, the wheel on the inside of the axle travels a shorter distance than the wheel on the outside. To achieve this a system of intermeshing pinions and ring gears enables the car to maintain its balance by turning the wheels at different speeds.

This metaphor can help us understand the logic behind equal opportunities. It is a question not of discriminating in favor of one wheel against another but of tuning each so as to harmonize them all. Just as a car keeps on the road when negotiating turns, so we must ensure that the Republic and its values also hold the road. To put it another way, giving due weight to diversity in the employment policies of public services has to be good for those services in all parts of the city. So, the more we create selective measures to correct inequalities between different population groups, the more vital it is that we are completely scrupulous in requiring candidates from disadvantaged neighborhoods or of immigrant origin to be properly qualified. Bearing in mind what is at stake psychologically when a student from a lycée in the hoods enters a grande école such as Sciences Po, there must be no special favors in the selection process. Here, perhaps more than anywhere else, casting errors will simply play into the hands of those who are opposed to the blending machine we need.

Lessons from the Transport Sector

It is worth mentioning here forms of social blending engineered in the transport sector during the 1990s.[15] Faced with the serious degradation of operating conditions in the hoods and recurring temptations to boycott such areas, public transport operators tried to adjust their services to overcome these difficulties. They put mediators on buses, subway cars, and trams to reassure passengers who felt insecure. Then, gradually, to improve social cohesion across the city, they introduced training programs for drivers and inspectors to help them better handle the violence to which they were exposed. In the early 1990s the Paris subway authority even sent what amounted to missionaries out into the hoods. Elsewhere transport authorities sponsored sociocultural and sports programs for youths in the hoods, hired subcontractors employing workers from the hoods, and collaborated with municipal councils in coordinated action plans for improved social cohesion. The idea behind these initiatives was to generate a message of identification, transforming an object seen vaguely by youths in the hoods as "the state's bus" into a public object belonging at one and the same time to everyone and to no single individual.

The transport authorities' new approach thus consisted of developing personal contact with these youths to change their image of public transport and give a human face to those providing it. It was a matter not of engaging in positive discrimination in favor of young ethnics but of finding solutions to the incivilities and violence from which staff and equipment were suffering. These initiatives were not some kind of ethnic charity but a modern approach to managing public services in today's urban environment.

Efforts to recruit more staff from within ethnically marked neighborhoods helped change the mentalities and cultures of public service organizations. Today no one is surprised to see an Arab or a black bus driver. And when a driver puts on the company uniform—this is also true for other uniformed public services such as the police, firefighters, and postal workers—he is less likely to be ethnicized in "native" French eyes. Uniforms of this kind can, in effect, help dispel prejudices and reduce social anxieties.

There are clearly many merits in employment policies that stretch across differences of ethnicity and color. But we need the right tools to put such policies in place. One such tool is ethnic monitoring, which in France is hampered by serious ethical problems and barriers of political correctness.

7 Counting Origins

While greater social mixing is certainly needed, ethnic monitoring is no easy matter. In the United States, besides the problems associated with quotas, there are serious difficulties concerning the definition of ethnic groups and the extent to which particular individuals belong to one group rather than another. Among all those categorized as *Hispanic* how can account be taken of different forms of past discrimination suffered by minority groups as diverse as Puerto Ricans, Mexicans, Cubans, and Colombians? Similarly, among those categorized as *Asian*, how are we to distinguish between Chinese, Japanese, Filipinos, Koreans, and Vietnamese?

There is another problem: How should a person from mixed ethnic origins be classified? What about a child with a black father and a white mother?

It is impossible to count clearly without someone feeling unjustly treated. Difficulties of this kind have, in recent years, helped push affirmative action into a third phase, that of the dismantling of ethnic quotas. North American lawmakers now prefer forms of *positive action* that are more flexible and limited in scope. Affirmative action certainly has not abolished the racial and ethnic frontiers fragmenting American society, and it has benefited the poor less than the middle classes. But it has, nevertheless, helped produce greater social mixing by facilitating upward mobility in every sphere of public life by individuals of minority origin, who have become strongly patriotic Americans. We in France need to reflect dispassionately and without prejudice on the American experience in order to create new ways of ensuring equal opportunities for young ethnics.

Affirmative action targeting racial or ethnic minorities has been increasingly challenged and replaced by a spatially defined approach targeting disadvantaged areas. Here we can see the beginnings of a convergence between French and American approaches to equal opportunities.[1] To counter the decline in enrollments by black and Hispanic students following the removal of affirmative action measures, a state law adopted in Texas in 1997 required public universities to admit every year the top 10 percent of students from every high school in the state. Florida has introduced similar measures.

In France specific measures targeting discrimination against specific minorities have the disadvantage of reinforcing those minorities' social marginalization, if not their ghettoization. For this reason it is better for equal opportunities policies to target all socially disadvantaged persons, not just young ethnics. Spatially based policies targeting disadvantaged urban areas should take precedence over ethnically targeted policies. Antidiscrimination policy should put areas of this kind before specific ethnic groups. It is very difficult to conceive of policies being adopted in France aimed at correcting social inequalities targeting exclusively people of foreign origin and openly excluding native French citizens in similar situations. There is widespread political agreement that one form of discrimination cannot be corrected by creating another.

That said, it still remains essential for us in France to introduce a system of *counting differences* if we are to make a reality of equal opportunities. For spatial and ethnic approaches are complementary rather than contradictory. Sooner or later we will have to give the statistical means to an ombudsman for equal opportunities to measure the extent to which diversity is being achieved within the public sector. As victims of multiple forms of color-based discrimination, young ethnics will have to be identified statistically in terms of the features by which they are handicapped in the field of equal opportunities. Our nation needs the technical and legal means with which to compile statistics on ethnic origins. Too much time has already been lost. We can no longer leave to market forces and the abstract principle of universalism the management of de facto inequalities between citizens. State intervention must permanently guarantee that unjustified differentials will be corrected and that equality of opportunity will be ensured by monitoring the situation and retuning as necessary. To achieve this it is essential that we *quantify* the progress made in diversifying the labor force.

There can, of course, be no question of forcing onto

citizens any sort of system for keeping files or spying on them. If we explain clearly enough the objectives of these measures, job applicants and employers will voluntarily provide the necessary information on their origins, knowing that the information will be used to correct defects in the system so that equal opportunities can be better assured by seeking the causes of unequal treatment and eradicating injustices. Statistics on ethnic origins are a vital tool in producing a fairer social system that people can believe in. On the forms where people are to state their origins, provision should be made for those who do not wish to reply to this type of question to indicate this by checking a box accordingly.

The absence of statistical data on ethnic origins stands in the way of public action designed to correct inequalities. When you ask the human resource departments of public services, "How many of 'them' do you have?" they don't know what to answer because they have no way of counting employees according to their origins. This point came out clearly, for example, in two special numbers of the magazine GEND'*info*, published by the Gendarmerie nationale, the national paramilitary police service, in December 2000 and January 2001 on the topic "integration issues."[2] Asked what measures were being taken by the gendarmerie to facilitate the integration of personnel of foreign origin, the head of human resources replied:

To suppose that specific measures are taken in favor of one or more categories of personnel determined by differences of origin is to accept the idea that a certain form of segregation, albeit positive, exists within the gendarmerie. That is not our way of doing things, nor has it ever been, for such an approach would run counter to the republican ethic. A gendarme is first and foremost a citizen. He has rights and duties that must be respected in a spirit of mutual consideration. There can never be any question of a gendarme, whose primary mission is to ensure that the law is respected, behaving within the institution of which he is part in a way that would run counter to the law. The powers vested in commanders and the regulatory framework for indicting and correcting any departure from those norms are sufficient to protect the principles of equality, which must remain as they are in the handling of personnel matters.

He added that the gendarmerie maintained no list or file detailing personnel of foreign origin:

My concern is solely to deal with military police officers who enter our ranks after passing the appropriate and very precise selection tests. At no level in the chain of command can there be any form of discrimination between one category or another based on criteria relating to origin, ethnicity, religion, or beliefs.[3]

If we try to estimate the size of minority groups on the basis of officers' names, this is, of course, a very rough-and-ready approach. Out of curiosity I took a look at the 2004 directory of police superintendents and found about a dozen Maghrebi-sounding names out of a total of around eighteen thousand, that is to say, less than 1 percent! So what? What can be deduced from this? One of two things: either we reaffirm that the entry exam to the rank of police superintendent is open to everyone, provided that they are French citizens and have the necessary qualifications, and nothing needs to be changed, or we say that the number of superintendents of Maghrebi, African, Turkish, of Caribbean origin is too low in relation to an employment policy committed to diversity, in which case new recruitment methods need to be introduced. The point needs to be made that, for the police, the intelligence services (very particularly), and the gendarmerie, greater diversity in recruitment carries very direct benefits for the profession: with officers of diverse origins and colors, the security forces have the means to penetrate every part of society and to conduct effective investigations supported by multilingual officers, etc. Although true, this argument is insufficient on its own to persuade the national police force and the gendarmerie to pursue policies aimed at improving diversity in their ranks. As there is no official way of counting officers on the basis of their origins, there is no willingness to take concrete steps toward greater diversity and seemingly no political will to make fundamental changes to the system.

The idea of drawing statistical distinctions on the basis of origins always makes people feel ill at ease in France. There have, indeed, been major controversies among demographers generated by opponents of such distinctions.[4] Yet the fact remains that, if we are serious about equal opportunities, poking around in a broken motor without the proper tools is a pretty risky proposition, if not an outright con game. In line with the image of the differential we need the right kind of toolbox. When the elevator of social mobility has broken down, we need, not a lucky charm, or a republican incantation, but tools that will get it working again.

A final word on this. There is no reason why anyone, in the United States or France, should be ashamed of stating his or her origins. On the contrary I tend to think that there is always a feeling of pride when people are asked about their origins. Today young ethnics refuse to be ashamed of their origins. They no longer hide them. On the contrary the pendulum of identity politics is swinging in the direction of ostentatious displays of origins in the public arena.

Conclusion

Get Moving!

Public institutions must take their share of the blame for the failure of the so-called French model of integration. They can no longer survive on the basis of a republican sclerosis wrapped up in mythical past glories, for the lofty ideal of meritocracy has long since been rent asunder by the reality of racial discrimination. It is now an understatement to say that not everyone has equal access to the elevator of social mobility. Far too many people don't even know of its existence. As it simply isn't part of their mental geography, they have no means of accessing it.

We need to be vigorous and courageous in irrigating the paths to social mobility by *actively going in search* of citizens outside the system and diversifying public service personnel. France has entered a new turn in its history. The turn this time is a hairpin. An effective equal opportunities policy is one of the last chances open to us. We must use the nation's *differential* to enable it to stay on the road. Only thus can we secure the nation's future and avert the nightmare of its collapse into warring ethnic communities.

Public institutions are not the only ones to blame for these tensions. Young ethnics also need to take responsibility as individuals. They must *start to move*. Often they are reluctant to leave the hood, their family, their home, if they are offered a job away from their cocoon. They are frightened of being uprooted, frightened of being on their own, frightened of having to face themselves. This is an important problem limiting their access to the world of work. It is true that asking them to *dérouiller* means asking them to take a leap without any guarantee of a safe landing on the other side. It means asking them to come out of their shells, out of themselves. We have to speak pragmatically and assert the importance of people taking personal responsibility in a society that tends to defer to social workers, with the attendant risk of stifling the inner resources of individuals. *Dérouiller* means the opposite of standing like the base of a crane, rooted to a spot outside your apartment block. *Dérouiller* means *moving* to *make good*, taking risks by casting off your anchors, crossing symbolically to the other side of the tracks. It means exposing yourself to danger by getting close up to others. It means being ready to change in the process of meeting others.

Of course young ethnics in the hoods are not the only ones worried by what is unfamiliar, far off, and different. In a more general sense, in recent decades as cities have grown in size, the idea of striking out, leaving familiar territory, has become a source of anxiety. When feelings of insecurity grow, the tendency to remain with your own kind, on the spot, to minimize the risk of unpleasant encounters outweighs the spirit of adventure. The horizons within which you see yourself shrink. This kind of process has built especially high mental barriers among disadvantaged groups and among young ethnics in particular because of the microterritorialization in which they have immured themselves in recent years. To avoid this constant return to their own kind we have to educate them to "get moving," not in a negative sense, but, rather, in the positive sense of taking a look elsewhere—and, in the process, taking a look at themselves, for I am convinced that it is only when you move, when you travel, that you find yourself. You become free when you step outside your inner walls. The tendency of young ethnics to turn in on themselves geographically and mentally needs to be countered by the idea of travel as an alternative to the safe haven. This isn't necessarily easy. As Jamel Debbouze puts it, our message to these young people could be: "You have no chance—grab it!" Humor is often the most telling way of expressing deep truths.

Travel versus the safe haven: that is how we should read the attempts made by Sciences Po to irrigate its recruitment field so as to better attract talented youngsters from the hoods. These were courageous, pioneering, productive efforts. They have set off a positive chain reaction in our society. They have launched a momentum that has already achieved manifest successes that are a credit to the Republic. Now I know that high school students in the hoods have registered in their mental geography and, more precisely, in their geography of accessible places the address of that famed institute in Paris. Even in the Lycée Robert Doisneau in Vaulx-en-Velin, where Khaled Kelkal lived before his death, they have now heard of the rue Saint Guillaume, home of Sciences Po. Psychologically high school students in the ZEPS are now thinking in terms of positive role models and "why not me?" whereas only a few years earlier their thinking was "that's not for me, I don't belong there!"

Media coverage of this new mode of entry to Sciences Po and the numerous television debates to which it has given rise during the last few years have helped spread by word of mouth the discovery of this new terra incognita. Other grandes écoles have been quick to follow Sciences Po. These initiatives have breathed new life into the democratic values of our country after a quarter century of the empty and misleading discourse of integration. To look on the bright side let us say that those wasted years have at least now enabled us to chart a better course.

What does the future hold? I believe that, in the coming years, a culture of mobility, radical change, and risk taking will lead many young ethnics in the hoods to choose to live in ever wider spaces instead of continuing to internalize their stigmatization and hunker down in the hallways of their apartment blocks. There seems no way in which France can avoid this schism in the social geography of the banlieues. The seeds of the future have already been sown in many ways, though we can still hope to salvage something by implementing an equal opportunities policy that will genuinely benefit ethnically marked citizens.

It is now twenty years since I published my autobiographical narrative, *Le Gone du Chaâba*, which told the tale of how the Republic's school system enabled me to blossom during the early years of the Beur generation. Today I often receive letters of thanks from people I met in their classrooms when they were thirteen or fourteen years old. They are now adults and parents. Some stop me in the street in the towns where I'm invited to speak and tell me passionately how affected they were by my message about the importance of reading when they were looking for a sense of direction. Fortunately, for them, despite the difficult material conditions encountered in their families and neighborhoods, social determinism did not reign supreme. They have left the hoods, and, when possible, they have gotten their families out too. For them the world didn't stop on the other side of the tracks or even at the borders of France. They went much further. In the hoods tales of *très grands dérouilleurs* [megamovers] have become legendary in recent years. Those grand voyagers are young ethnics who traveled great distances to work, study, see other countries, follow a spouse, or simply breathe fresh air. Their traces are now everywhere. A Beur diaspora now exists. Or rather, we can say, a diaspora of former inhabitants of the hoods. These pioneers are now all over the world, in Australia, in America, in the Caribbean, in New Caledonia, in Guyana, echoing the voyages of their parents or grandparents when they fled the poverty of their native lands. Today a mere mention of the names of those mythical, far-off countries—America, Australia, New Caledonia—is sufficient to spark new dreams in the minds of many youths in the hoods. Legends of megamovers are themselves sufficient to open up new horizons and geographic frontiers. This is bringing new spheres of activity into the range of young men and women in the hoods, no longer simply along the axis linking the urban periphery to downtown, but also along an axis leading from the banlieues to Europe and the world as a whole. The Internet revolution is by no means unconnected with these globalized projections of the self. The information society has already begun to bring major changes to the lives of people living in the hoods as it has elsewhere. The information society generates forms of participation, both virtual and real, across spaces that know no boundaries. France needs to take heed of these forms of emigration. The most dynamic, creative, and courageous young ethnics emerging in the hoods have the world in their sights. They no longer see themselves condemned to remain the children of immigrants, descendants of colonized peoples, or recipients of the minimum wage. There is no longer any point in telling them stories of integration. They are clear-sighted. More and more of them are leaving so that the rest of the world can benefit from their talents and skills, for elsewhere in the world there are still countries—and this is no myth—where the only things that matter in determining social recognition are the personal merits of individuals.

MAY 2005

Notes

Translator's Introduction

1. "Azouz Begag, principal opposant à Nicolas Sarkozy," *Le Monde*, November 2, 2005.

2. Begag's *Le Gone du Chaâba* (Paris: Seuil, 1986) has been translated by Naïma Wolf and Alec G. Hargreaves as *Shantytown Kid* (Lincoln: University of Nebraska Press, 2007).

3. The earlier book is Azouz Begag, *Les Dérouilleurs: Ces Français de banlieue qui ont réussi* (Paris: Mille et une nuits, 2002). On the so-called beurgeoisie, see Catherine Wihtol de Wenden and Rémy Leveau, *La Beurgeoisie: Les trois ages de la vie associative issue de l'immigration* (Paris: CNRS Editions, 2001).

4. The details of French nationality laws are complex, but in broad terms they endow French citizenship automatically on the children and grandchildren of immigrants. Persons born in France of foreign parents generally become French at

the age of eighteen; the children of immigrants from Algeria, regarded as an integral part of France during the colonial period, are French from birth, as is any person born in France who also has at least one parent born in France.

5. "M. Chevènement annonce un renforcement de la lutte contre les violences urbaines," *Le Monde*, March 11, 1998; "M. Chevènement reprend sa croisade contre la délinquance des mineurs," *Le Monde*, January 12, 1999.

6. "Le visiteur," *Libération*, October 28, 2005; "Emeutes de Clichy-sous-Bois: Les interventions de Nicolas Sarkozy sont contestées, même à droite," *Le Monde*, November 1, 2005.

7. Béatrice Gurrey, "Jacques Chirac affirme qu'il a pris 'toutes les mesures nécessaires' sur la crise des banlieues," *Le Monde*, November 12, 2005.

8. It has not been forgotten among minority ethnic groups that, in colonial Algeria, those formally designated as Muslims were explicitly characterized by the state as noncitizens, deprived of voting and other rights, and subject to discretionary administrative powers that, in many respects, placed them beyond the protection of the law.

In colonial times, those designated as *natives* [*indigènes*] were non-Europeans subject to colonial rule. The word was transposed to the situation of minorities in contemporary France by signatories of a 2005 manifesto on behalf of those it called *les indigènes de la République* [lit. "the Republic's natives"] (see "Nous, 'indigènes de la République,'" *Le Monde*, March 17, 2005).

9. The subsequent adoption of this term in the mass media, where it became closely associated with the stigmatized banlieues, led many second-generation Maghrebis to reject the *Beur* label. See Sylvie Durmelat, "Petite histoire du mot 'beur,'" *French Cultural Studies* 9, no. 2 (June 1998): 191–207.

10. See, e.g., Michèle Tribalat, *De l'immigration à l'assimilation:*

Enquête sur les populations d'origine immigrée (Paris: La Découverte/INED, 1996).

11. Alec G. Hargreaves, "Half-Measures: Anti-Discrimination Policy in France," *French Politics, Culture, and Society* 18, no. 3 (Fall 2000): 83-101; Erik Bleich, *Race Politics in Britain and France: Ideas and Policymaking since the 1960s* (Cambridge: Cambridge University Press, 2003).

Author's Preface

1. A provision inserted into the draft law in January 2006 at the initiative of Prime Minister Dominique de Villepin aimed to reduce youth unemployment through greater labor market flexibility. It was hoped that employers would be more willing to hire young workers if they could also fire them more easily. Following nationwide protests by students and trade unions, the easy hire–easy fire proposal was dropped and, in April 2006, replaced by targeted incentives encouraging employers to hire youths with low levels of certified skills in disadvantaged neighborhoods, prominent among whom were those whom Begag calls *young ethnics*.—Trans.

1. Fear of the Police

1. On the Arab quarter of Lyon, see Azouz Begag, *Place du Pont ou la médina de Lyon* (Paris: Autrement, 1997).

2. The German sociologist Georg Simmel first formulated his concept of the *stranger* in a 1908 essay translated into English as "The Sociological Significance of the 'Stranger,'" in *Introduction to the Science of Sociology*, ed. Robert E. Park and Ernest W. Burgess (Chicago: University of Chicago Press, 1921), 322-27.—Trans.

3. On the neglect of antidiscrimination policy, see Véronique de Rudder, Christian Poiret, and François Vourc'h, *L'Inégalité raciste: L'universalité républicaine à l'épreuve* (Paris: Presses Universitaires de France, 2000).

4. "Une 'rafle' contre de jeunes Maghrébins au parc départemental de Nanterre," *Le Monde*, June 10–11, 1980.

5. "Bron: Les méthodes policières en question; un collectif d'associations dénonce l'attitude de certains policiers vis-à-vis des jeunes," *Le Progrès de Lyon*, June 22, 1979.

6. "Parce qu'Azzedine avait frappé le commissaire," *Témoignage chrétien*, April 7, 1980.

7. Mogniss, "Jeunes immigrés hors les murs," *Questions clefs*, no. 2 (1982): 53.

8. An exception was October 17, 1961, when Algerian immigrants demonstrated in Paris in favor of Algerian independence and found in their path the Paris chief of police, Maurice Papon. Scores, perhaps hundreds, of them were killed that night.

9. By *dérouilleurs* I mean young people from the hoods who have achieved social success.

10. Yazid Kherfi and Véronique Le Goaziou, *Repris de justesse* (Paris: Syros, 2000), 59.

11. A ZEP is a *zone d'éducation prioritaire*, i.e., a disadvantaged area containing schools targeted for special support.—Trans.

12. See the novel by Y. B., *Allah superstar* (Paris: Grasset, 2003).

13. Azouz Begag, "La République à ciel ouvert" (Report for the Minister of the Interior, November 2004).

14. Norbert Elias and John L. Scotson, *The Established and the Outsiders: A Sociological Enquiry into Community Problems*, 2nd ed. (London: Sage, 1994), 129.

2. Identity Comes and Goes

1. After the 9/11 attacks, Sikhs were assaulted in a number of American cities because their turbans were mistakenly taken to signify that they were Muslims.

2. Even when traveling on a diplomatic passport following his appointment as a French government minister, Begag was subjected to similar treatment by the U.S. authorities at the Atlanta airport in the fall of 2005. See "Le ministre français

Azouz Begag a fait l'objet d'un contrôle 'poussé' à l'aéroport d'Atlanta," *Le Monde*, October 25, 2005.—Trans.

3. Begag is here parodying a famous line from Molière's *Tartuffe*: "Cachez ce sein que je ne saurais voir!" [Remove this breast from my sight, for upon it my eyes should not alight!].—Trans.

3. Disintegration

1. See Elias and Scotson, *The Established and the Outsiders*.

2. I first sketched out this typology in "Entre 'rouiller' et 's'arracher': Réapprendre à flâner," *Annales de la recherche urbaine*, nos. 59-60 (September 1993): 179–88.

3. James Baldwin, *The Fire Next Time* (New York: Dial, 1963).

4. *Cailleras* is a *verlan* [back slang] expression for *racaille* [scum].—Trans.

5. CLARIS, "La dérive ethnique," *Libération*, April 5, 2005.

6. In all honesty I must acknowledge that I recently gave a lecture in a hood where people told me that this isn't true any more. There are realtors who give fake reasons for refusing to sell properties to ethnically marked clients. If so, we are heading toward even worse, hermetically sealed forms of segregation.

7. See Wihtol de Wenden and Leveau, *La Beurgeoisie*.

8. Ariane Chemin, "L'élite 'beure' mène le débat sur les minorités . . . hors des partis," *Le Monde*, February 20, 2005.

4. I Exists

1. The Centre National de la Recherche Scientifique, a state-funded agency for research.—Trans.

2. See Cornelius Castoriadis, *L'Institution imaginaire de la société* (Paris: Seuil, 1975).

3. On learning to learn, see Gaston Bachelard, *La Formation de l'esprit scientifique* (Paris: J. Vrin, 1977).

4. "Moi, Khaled Kelkal," *Le Monde*, October 7, 1995.

5. See Malcolm X, *February 1965: The Final Speeches* (New York: Pathfinder, 1992).

5. We *Are Stronger Than* You

1. Begag, *Les Dérouilleurs*, 112–13.
2. Ibid., 117-18.
3. "Manifestations de lycéens: Le spectre des violences anti-'blancs,'" *Le Monde*, March 16, 2005. Sevran and Montreuil are in the northeastern and eastern banlieues of Paris.
4. Similar tensions are experienced by those who work as mediators in urban public transport systems. See Azouz Begag and Reynald Rossini, *Du bon usage de la distance chez les sauvageons* (Paris: Seuil, 1999).

6. Equal Opportunities

1. The word *sauvageons* was used in 1998 and 1999 by the socialist interior minister, Jean-Pierre Chevènement, to describe disruptive youths in the banlieues.—Trans.
2. "S'en prendre à un blanc gâté, ça existe," *Libération*, April 16–17, 2005.
3. See Pierre Bourdieu, *La Distinction: Critique sociale du jugement* (Paris: Minuit, 1979).
4. The most successful are often those who, like the children of teachers, are "bathed" in knowledge, giving them "natural" access to codes of knowledge.
5. Discrimination in this sector is based on the premise that an Arab or a black is bad for sales, which is not necessarily true if the Arabs or blacks are successful athletes or musicians.
6. Kabyles are the largest of the Berber-speaking minorities in Algeria, where the majority of the population are Arabs.—Trans.
7. See Yazid Sebag and Laurence Méhaignerie, *Les Oubliés de l'égalité des chances* (Paris: Institut Montaigne, 2004).
8. I am deliberately using the words *Arabs, Muslims,* and *immi-*

grants together here because, in French public opinion, Arabs, Muslims, and immigrants—and, indeed, terrorists and Islamists—all evoke similar images.

9. Today it is increasingly common to hear ordinary people say that they afraid of using the word *Arab* because it is perceived as pejorative, as an insult. They are often unable to distinguish between Arabs and Muslims, immigrants and Maghrebis.

10. Raffarin was prime minister from 2002 to 2005.—Trans.

11. Notwithstanding the fears mentioned earlier (see n. 9 above), many ordinary people still call these people *Arabs*.

12. This point is forcefully made in a manifesto entitled "Nous les indigènes de la République!" (http://toutesegaux.free.fr/article.php3?id–article=90).

13. I have tried to assist in this process in some of my literary works, such as *Un Train pour chez nous* (Paris: Thierry Magnier, 2001) and *Le Marteau pique-coeur* (Paris: Seuil, 2004). From the age of seven on, for the best part of twenty years, I went on holiday every summer to the native village of my parents near Sétif, in northeastern Algeria. Every time I felt the lingering imprint of the colonial past and the military conquest on which it was based, the ghost of my friend Sergeant Blandan. In *Le Marteau-piqueur*, I write of Sétif:

> Twenty years ago I accompanied my father on a visit to see some old friends with whom he shared memories of events such as those of May 1945, when the French army shot indiscriminately at the local Arabs. My father and his friends had lain flat in the wheat fields. Some of the soldiers saw them and fired into the fields to try to flush them out. After the shooting stopped, one of their friends failed to emerge from the fields. They went to look for him and were relieved to find him easily, for he hadn't moved. But that was the problem. He was past moving. There were two holes in his head, which the flies were busily using as a larder and

playground. The story dates from May 8, 1945. My father never forgot that day. The French colonial regime was not at all happy with the state of affairs in that backwater of the empire, so it had sent in its soldiers to chastise all the Muslims and remind them who was in charge.... This was one of the few stories I managed to get out of my father while he was alive. On everything else it was a case of ask no questions: his lips were sealed.

As we left the Kherrata ravine, on the side of one of the towering mountains one could read: "Foreign Legion, 1945." French Algeria was tattooed everywhere in this region, in the wheat fields, in the rocks, in people's memories.

And in El-Ouricia [my parents' native village] too. My parents had spent a sizable part of their lives on a farm working at the beck and call of the rich settler who owned it. We children had accompanied them on several pilgrimages there. Every time they remembered exactly what the place had been like, how it felt, the settler's bedroom, the kitchen where my mother had worked, the tree on which she hung the *chekoua*, a goatskin full of sheep's or cow's milk that she would shake to make butter, the stable where the horses were better treated than they were, the sitting room where she waited on the settler's wife. To get to the farm you followed a long track bordered by oak trees at the end of which was an impressive gate that now could only be imagined for it had long since been stolen amid the fiesta that marked the end of the colonial era. (161–63)

14. Bruno Caussé, "Le chantre de la discrimination positive," *Le Monde*, April 3, 1997, supplement "Vivre Lyon."

15. See Begag and Rossini, *Du bon usage*.

7. Counting Origins

1. See Patrick Simon and Daniel Sabbagh, "Discrimination pos-

itive et déségrégation," *Sociétés contemporaines*, no. 53 (June 2004): 94.

2. "Questions d'intégration," GEND'*info*, nos. 231 (December 2000) and 232 (January 2001).

3. GEND'*info*, no. 231, pp. 19, 14.

4. See Maryse Tripier, "De l'usage de statistiques 'ethniques,'" *Hommes et migrations*, no. 1219 (May–June 1999): 27–31; Patrick Simon and Joan Stavo-Debauge, *Les Discriminations raciales et statistiques: À la recherche d'une cohérence* (Paris: FASILD, 2002); and Patrick Simon, *Les Discriminations ethniques dans la société française: Une synthèse* (Paris: IHESI, 2000).

Glossary

banlieues Lit. "suburbs"; since the 1980s has been widely used to denote disadvantaged urban areas with dense concentrations of minority ethnic inhabitants.

beurgeoisie A play on the words *Beurs* (s.v.) and *bourgeoisie*; the former denotes second-generation Maghrebis (s.v.), generally at the lower end of the socioeconomic ladder, in contrast with the latter, a more affluent and powerful social class.

Beurs Second-generation Maghrebis (s.v.), who, unlike their immigrant parents, were born in France.

cailleras Verlan (s.v.) form of *racaille* (s.v.).

cités Lit. "urban neighborhoods"; in contemporary usage denotes working-class neighborhoods, especially those containing high concentrations of social housing and minority ethnic residents, similar to those known in the United States as "housing projects" or, colloquially, as "hoods."

cnrs   Centre National de la Recherche Scientifique, national state-funded agency for research.

collège   Junior high school.

communautarisme   Ethnic separatism or factionalism.

député   Member of the National Assembly, the lower chamber of the French parliament.

dérouilleurs   Neologism invented by Begag derived antithetically from the verb *rouiller* [to rust], denoting inhabitants of the banlieues (s.v.) who, instead of rotting where they are, achieve social mobility; can be loosely translated as "movers."

Front National   Extreme-right, anti-immigration political party led by Jean-Marie Le Pen.

gendarmes   Paramilitary police officers under the jurisdiction of the Defense Ministry but under the operational control of the Interior Ministry.

grandes écoles   Higher education institutions with competitive entrance examinations; more prestigious than regular French universities, they are the entranceways to elite career paths. They include the Ecole Nationale d'Administration [National Administration College], which trains senior civil servants, and the Institut d'Etudes Politiques de Paris [Political Science Institute of Paris], popularly known as Sciences Po.

grands frères   Lit. "older brothers"; often serves to denote older second-generation Maghrebis (s.v.) who try to advise and guide less experienced youngsters.

halal   Meat that conforms with Islamic dietary prescriptions.

harkis   Muslim soldiers who fought on the side of the French against Algerian nationalists during the Algerian war of independence (1954–62).

imam   Muslim prayer leader.

keufs   Verlan (s.v.) expression formed by inverting the syllables of *flics*, meaning "cops."

khobz ed'dar   Arabic for homemade bread.

Le Pen, Jean-Marie   Leader of the Front National (s.v.) party.

lycée   Senior high school.

Maghrebis   North Africans (in French, *Maghrébins, Nord-Africains*).

petit-blanc   Poor white.

pieds-noirs   European settlers in French North Africa, most of whom fled to France with the independence of Algeria in 1962.

prefect   Civil servant (in French, *préfet*) representing France's central government at the level of the *département*, roughly equivalent to a county in the United States.

quartiers sensibles   Lit. "sensitive" or "fragile" neighborhoods; often abbreviated to *quartiers*; equivalent to urban areas known colloquially in the United States as "hoods."

racaille   Scum.

Rebeus   Second-generation North Africans; verlan (s.v.) version of *Beurs* (s.v.), itself an inversion of *Arabes*.

renois   Blacks; verlan (s.v.) for *noirs*.

rouilleurs   Neologism invented by Begag derived from the verb *rouiller* [to rust], denoting young inhabitants of the banlieues (s.v.) who fail to seek or secure social mobility and rot where they are.

sauvageons   Wild children or young savages.

trente glorieues   Thirty years of sustained economic growth ending in the mid-1970s.

verlan   Back slang.

ZEP   *Zone d'éducation prioritaire*; a disadvantaged neighborhood containing schools targeted for special support.

ZUP   *Zone à urbaniser en priorité*; mainly low-income urban area containing dense concentrations of social housing.

Index

Lyon (*cont.*)
110; geographical region of, 52–53; schools/education in, 27, 28, 60; ZUPS in, 14

Magellan, Ferdinand, 71
Maghreb, as French North Africa, ix
Maghrebis: and deportations of Maghrebi youth, xxvii, xxviii, 12, 17, 18; as economic scapegoats, 12; French generations of, xvii, 4, 20, 130n9; Kabyles in, 102, 134n6; social practices of, 56–57. *See also* young ethnics
maille, 44
Malcolm X, 75
Maleh, Gad El, 57
Marche des Beurs, xxvi, 17, 85, 88
March on Washington, 17
Le Mas du Taureau, 52
Mékachéra, Hamlaoui, 107
meritocracy, 96, 123
métro-boulot-dodo, 52
Les Minguettes, 14, 15, 52
minorities, third generation of, ix–x
Mitterrand, François, 15, 17
mobility: economic autonomy and, 79–81; loss of, 68–69; social, 120; vertical, 92; young ethnics with, 92–114

Le Monde, 73
money: buying freedom with, 69; function of, 44, 45–46; social emancipation and, 79–81
multiculturalism, 37–38
Muslim, label of, 20, 86–87

Nantes Business School, 106
National Aeronautics and Space Administration (NASA), 74
National Assembly, 53, 107, 108
nationality laws, xv, 129–30n4
Nation of Islam, 75
nihilism, 47
noirs, 20
North Africa: forced repatriations to, xxvii; historic battles in, 28–29, 108; Muslim populations in, vii, 129, nn8–9. *See also* Algeria; Maghreb
nouveaux riches, 46

oil, price of, 11
omerta, 42
Oran, 29
Organization of Petroleum Exporting Countries (OPEC), 11
the Other, 11, 51, 63, 82, 95
Oued Radjett, 108

UNIVERSITY OF NEBRASKA PRESS